Hair Raising

Hair Raising

BEAUTY, CULTURE, AND
AFRICAN AMERICAN WOMEN

NOLIWE M. ROOKS

RUTGERS UNIVERSITY PRESS
New Brunswick, New Jersey

Library of Congress Cataloging-in-Publication Data
Rooks, Noliwe M., 1963–
Hair raising : beauty, culture, and African American women /
Noliwe Rooks.
p. cm.   Includes bibliographical references and index.
ISBN 0-8135-2311-7 (cloth : alk. paper). — ISBN 0-8135-2312-5
(pbk. : alk. paper)
1. Hairdressing of Afro-Americans—History.   2. Beauty culture—
United States—History.   3. Afro-American women—History.
I. Title.
TT972.R66   1996
391'.5'08996073—dc20   95-51395

British Cataloging-in-Publication information available

Published by Rutgers University Press, New Brunswick, New Jersey
Manufactured in the United States of America

"Among the Things That Use to Be," by Willi M. Coleman, from
Home Girls: A Black Feminist Anthology, © 1983, reprinted by
permission of the author and Kitchen Table: Women of Color Press,
P.O. Box 40–4920, Brooklyn, NY 11240–4920.

For my grandmother, Evelyn Baker Rooks

1912–1993

Contents

Illustrations

Acknowledgments

When I began writing these acknowledgments, they very quickly got out of control. I thanked everyone (living and dead) I have ever known and cared about. Whereas these were wonderful sentiments, an endless list of "thank you for existing, thank you for listening, thank you for supporting me" does not make for interesting reading. Besides, the possibility of including every individual who had ever listened or supported me was, at best, remote. I decided to try to do a better job of telling most folks what they meant to me and just focus here on those without whom this project could not have come to fruition.

As an undergraduate, I attended Spelman College and had the privilege of taking classes with Beverly Guy-Sheftall, Judy Gebre-Hewitt, Paula Giddings, and Gloria Wade-Gayles. These women are *passionate* about the past and present lives, literatures, and histories of African American women. You taught me much more than you will ever know about the rewards of researching and writing about African American women and the possibilities in "claiming my intellectual space." Thank you.

At the University of Iowa, I had the good fortune of meeting Peter Byron Thornton, who, while helping me come up with a topic for a paper, suggested I write about black women and hair. Your idea was a gift that has helped me make sense of academia. Thank you.

Once I started work on this project, Karen Smith, Cherry Muhanji, Akilah Blackwomyn, and Tracy Cherry kept me sane (or at least gave it their best shot). They read and reread chapters, provided devastatingly accurate insights and criticisms, and made sure that I never took myself or my work too seriously. Y'all know you do/did much more than this, but I'll have to write another book to do you justice. Much love and thank you.

After I had spent some ungodly number of hours in the archives researching Walker's life, Wilma Gibbs, curator of the Madam C. J. Walker Collection at the Indiana Historical Society, took me home with her. She introduced me to her family, talked with me about the world, fed me, and took me to a shop that still sells Walker products. I now have a tangible piece of the history I worked on for so long. She also made it possible for me to speak with A'Lelia Bundles, Walker's great-great-grand-daughter, who is working on a definitive biography of Madam Walker's life. A'Lelia, I trust you know how much your support for this book means to me, and I hope that the two of you feel I have done justice to "the madam." Thank you.

When I first spoke with Rutgers's wonderfully thorough copy editor, Kathryn Gohl, she had recently completed work on this manuscript. She tried to prepare me for seeing my work with editorial questions, comments, and changes written in red. Little did she know that after having worked with my dissertation adviser, Lauren Rabinovitz, her corrections and suggestions were easy to take in stride. Lauren made my work look like a dissertation, and Kathryn made it look like a book. Lauren also introduced me to Leslie Mitchner, my editor at Rutgers University Press. I keep thinking that this book publishing thing is an almost effortless, pain-free process. I suspect that this has much to do with you three. Thank you.

My colleagues at the University of Missouri–Kansas City have been nothing but supportive and welcoming. Joan Dean, Lois Spatz, Mindy Fiala, and Marianne Wells have been particularly so. You made my transition to a new job and city easy by quickly inviting me into your minds and lives. What would I do without Monday night to look forward to. Thank you.

For as long as I can remember, my "auntie," Jean Wiley, has questioned, challenged, nurtured, and supported me. My mother, Belvie Rooks, has done all of the above and so much more. She is the only cheering section, publicist, historian, or conscience I could ever need. I am not surprised that y'all's questions, time, energy, and editorial suggestions for this manuscript in all its varying forms were the *most* crucial. I'm not quite sure what I, or it, would be without you. I love you madly and thank you.

1

Nappi by Nature

Afros, Hot Combs, and Black Pride

*I*n 1976 I was thirteen years old. I believed that the mix of spirituality and Afrocentrism in Earth, Wind, and Fire's lyrics was "deep." I yelled myself hoarse at my first live concert starring Bootsie Collins. I liked disco (does anyone remember Chic, and of course there was Donna Summer). I listened to Gil Scott Heron and *knew* "the revolution would not be televized" because I watched shows like "Good Times" and "The Jeffersons." I left home early every Saturday morning to sit through movies like *Sparkle* and *Aaron Loves Angela*. I discovered boys, makeup, and junior high school cliques (truly one of the most exclusive types of clubs with some of the most exacting standards of any group I have since come in contact with). I was an absolute adolescent. This was also the year I decided to straighten my hair. In the process of reaching my decision, I came to realize the extent to which my hair bridged the space between personal identity and a larger racial politic. Hair, I learned that year, is significant.

As I recall, the first (of many) major fights I had with my

mother had to do with my hair. I had never really paid mine any serious attention. Generally, I wore it pulled back in one or two Afro puffs, or sometimes I had it braided. In the black cultural world I inhabited, where much of my social life revolved around my mother and our extended family, natural hair was highly valued. We were cultural and political activists.

For example, I clearly remember the planning meetings for the San Francisco Bay Area's first African Liberation Day held in the early 1970s. The theme was "We are an African people." I understood the Black Panthers to be a community group committed to bettering the lives of working-class and poor African Americans because I saw and experienced the work they did. I could name all of the Soledad Brothers and the San Quentin Six and was allowed out of school for rallies to "free Angela Davis," who was incarcerated at the Marin County Jail. I still remember the few occasions I was allowed into the courtroom. I knew who Kwame Nkrumah, Amilcar Cabral, and Che Guevara were— not just their names and faces but what they believed, how their ideologies differed, and what made them revolutionaries. This was the year my mother seriously contemplated marrying a Zimbabwean who later became a minister in the new government, and I spent the summer before my fourteenth birthday in Cuba, at an international youth camp.

I was a black activist baby. If, as the African proverb says, "it takes a whole village to raise a child," then that child is a reflection of the values of the village. The community of people who saw me as a part of their responsibility to raise taught me that African Americans occupied a precarious position in relation to white culture and that everything from my name to my choice of hairstyle was a reflection on their parenting skills. We were of African descent and consciously proud of it. All that identified me more closely with Africa and other African Americans was good. Those things that spoke to valuing whiteness and denigrating our heritage were problematic. There was no way for my mother to understand my desire for straightened hair as anything other than a rejection of my "African" self and, therefore, as a capitulation to the values of the dominant culture. My desire for straight hair became a symbol of her failure and of my rejection of who she taught me to believe I was. I, however, saw things differently.

I had recently started a new school, and absolutely no one there wore their hair in a natural except me. I was determined to fit in with my new classmates—an insurgent community of thirteen-year-olds I desperately wanted to join. I knew that it would mean a fight with my mother and readied myself for it. As I prepared my arguments and worked on getting up my nerve, I cut out a number of magazine advertisements to show her the styles that interested me. Because the majority of my examples came from African American publications (*Essence, Jet, Ebony,* etc.), I believed they would "prove" that straight hair was indeed a part of African American culture and, as a result, a style I should be allowed to embrace. Besides, I reasoned, during one of my imaginary orations, it was my hair and at thirteen I wasn't sure I really needed to ask permission to change its style. My mother had had thirteen years to shape me into the person she wanted me to be; all I was doing was asking for an opportunity to begin the process of shaping myself. I believed my mother had generally been relatively reasonable and knew she valued intellect and persuasion, so I thought I had a shot at winning. I was wrong.

My mother said no, and for the next few days I received nonstop speeches on why my hair was fine the way it was as well as on the political implications of my even asking to change it. For her, there could be no true understanding of and pride in my ancestry if I chose to straighten my hair, and she voiced great concern regarding my self-esteem and beliefs about my identity in relation to the larger society. It became clear that whatever personal autonomy my mother wished to foster stopped short of supporting my desire for straight hair. The story, however, did not end there.

When I went South for the summer, my grandmother could not get me to Miss Ruby's beauty parlor and a straightening comb fast enough. My grandmother grounded her sanction of straightened hair in a politics of acceptance. She reasoned that because no one was ever going to mistake me for having anything other than African ancestry due to the dark color of my skin and because she understood America, particularly the American South, as a place where power had to be finessed as well as met head on, in confrontation, straightening my hair would give me an advantage in the world. It was one less battle that would have to be fought.

My grandmother was a card-carrying member of a pre-integration, southern, middle-class, African American community. She was a teacher in the city's only black school and married to the principal. Even though those positions gave them financial security and a degree of respect within their community, I grew up hearing stories of the threats, harassment, and physical confrontation that accompanied their efforts to unionize African American teachers across the South. One of the scariest stories was about the night white men with shotguns blasted out all of the windows in their home and the fear and rage she, my grandfather, and my father felt as they cowered on the floor.

My grandmother was a graduate of Bethune Cookman, historically a black college for women; a member of an African American sorority (Alpha Kappa Alpha); a trustee at the church she belonged to for thirty years; and a community leader. It was she who urged me to go to a black college, any black college, whereas my mother encouraged me to go to Sarah Lawrence, an exclusive, predominantly white, East Coast institution. My grandmother never believed she was white. As far as I know, she never privileged white culture. She always taught me to be proud of who I was and the people from whom I came. Although I did learn important, often disturbing lessons about class and how it can function to separate African Americans, my grandmother was clear that though successful, she was still very much a part of her community. The white community was always "other." For my grandmother, hair spoke to acceptance from a certain class of African Americans but had relatively little to do with white supremacy, Africa, or self-esteem.

As for me, I quickly discovered that Florida's heat and the accompanying sweat were not conducive to hair straightened with a hot comb. It "went back," or reverted to its natural state, rather quickly. It was also just plain more trouble than it was worth. I took to wearing my hair in cornrows for most of the summer—a style that satisfied both my mother's desire for a "natural" hairstyle and my grandmother's conception of acceptable hairstyling for an African American child. However, I reached this compromise reluctantly because I was hesitant to give up the experiences I associated with my trips to the beauty parlor.

I loved being in the waiting area (really just a few chairs clustered near the door) and listening to all the bits of advice and gossip that were flying about. Sitting in a room full of African American women and hearing them talk about sex, white people, men, and money, I got clues on how to be and how not to act. I loved the smell of the place. The mixture of burning hair, sweet-smelling shampoos, chemicals, food, and sweat (there was no air-conditioning, only a fan). I absolutely adored having someone wash my hair for me. The feel of hands massaging my scalp as they worked the shampoo in, rinsed, and rewashed until I heard the squeak that meant it was clean. I was so proud when Miss Ruby told me I had finally learned how to sit in the chair "right," not fidgeting and holding my ear down far enough so she wouldn't burn me with the hot straightening comb. I was absolutely fascinated by the way my hair looked when she finished: flat, shiny, smooth. I must admit there were times when I contemplated a career path that led me to where Miss Ruby stood.

In 1976, my desire for straight hair quickly became an intergenerational struggle that exposed both tensions and contradictions in my family and spoke to larger concerns with which African Americans in the mid-seventies were grappling. I was caught between competing definitions of Black Power, Black Community, and Black Pride. Whereas neither road led to a desire for whiteness or white culture, both routes led to very specific assumptions about my place in relation to other African

Americans and the larger white society. Hair in 1976 spoke to racial identity politics as well as bonding between African American women. Its style could lead to acceptance or rejection from certain groups and social classes, and its styling could provide the possibility of a career. What I envisioned as a personal statement of choice was clearly political and quite complicated.

This work is an attempt to unsnarl the various meanings of hair in African American culture. When I began to research and write about the politics of African American hair, I was primarily interested in the 1960s and '70s because I believed that what the Afro came to symbolize then was the beginning of the issues and contradiction I wanted to discuss. When I began, I thought I understood where the views and beliefs about hair that my grandmother, mother, and myself held came from, and how hair and the meaning of hair were impacted by political and historical shifts. I knew that as the Civil Rights Movement became the Black Liberation or Black Power Movement in the mid-seventies, wearing an Afro became synonymous with nationalist sentiments within both the African American community and America at large.

For example, although some may be unclear about who Angela Davis was and the particulars of why she was incarcerated, we remember her Afro—a halo of natural hair framing her face—and her closed fist raised in the Black Power salute. The Afro was understood to denote black pride, which became synonymous with activism and political consciousness. This sentiment moved sharply against the prevailing integrationist ideology and evidenced a belief that the gains of the Civil Rights Movement were not broad-based enough. It is perhaps this dichotomy that led Gloria Wade-Gayles to write that

> An activist with straight hair was a contradiction. A lie. A joke, really. The right to tout the movement gospel of self-esteem carried with it the obligation to accept and love one's self naturally. Our appearance had to speak the truth before our lips stretched to sing songs. Never again, I decided, would I alter

my hair. In its natural state, my hair would be a badge, a symbol of my self-esteem and racial pride. An act of genuine bonding with black women who were incarcerated in jails all across America and those who were in psychological jails, accepting less from everyone because they believed they deserved less than anyone. I decided to wear an Afro.[1]

However, even in the heyday of the Black Power movement, another writer would see things differently.

In a May 1963 *Liberator* article entitled "Hot Irons and Black Nationalism," Eleanor Mason, who wore her hair in an Afro, argued that folks tended to make too much of a connection between natural hair and liberation politics. She went on to add, "I have chosen to stand in the white man's emporium and challenge his values. I can walk in the jungle with my head high even if I choose to bleach my hair and cut my coat to resemble that of the Tiger; I shall always have a certain intrinsic worth which distinguishes me from him." Decades later, in yet another interpretation of natural hair politics, Alice Walker suggests that straightening one's hair is a form of oppression and that the act puts a "ceiling on the brain," thus keeping one from reaching spiritual growth and fulfillment.[2] Given these different interpretations of the Afro, it is not surprising that hair and the politics of hair appear frequently in contemporary writings by African American women.

Happi to Be Nappi: African American Women Writing about Hair

How important a space in African American women writers' texts are matters concerning hair? If not always as pervasive as Zora Neale Hurston's descriptions of Janie in *Their Eyes Were Watching God,* where, as Mary Helen Washington observes, "hair becomes another character in the novel,"[3] then matters attendant to the grade, style, and care of hair do seem to function as symbolic of a character's sense of identity, social status, health, and sense of purpose in African American culture. As with such metaphoric references as "mothers' gardens" or "grandma's quilt," oftentimes much more is represented than a mere material or anatomical feature, and as a rhetorical tool, the description of rituals associated with hair and its care often foreshadows the development of the protagonist.

In novels such as *Dessa Rose, Quicksand, Passing, The Color Purple, Mama Day,* and *The Bluest Eye,* hair is the site where African American women comb their memories and braid or straighten their experiences to express the dreams and possibilities of a social reality where they are equal partners in the creation and styling of a world free of oppression. Moreover, like history and literature, hair, even in what is presumed to be its "natural" state, is shaped by culturally determined creative and re-creative acts to form and further particular ends.

While a graduate student, I devoted much time to researching and discussing the politics of African American hair. In one class I learned how to conduct the ethnographic interview, a process whereby one goes into a community/place/town/ group of people and supposedly extracts information without allowing personal bias to get in the way. I chose one of two black beauty parlors in the nearby town as my site. What I learned in my fieldwork can be neatly summed up by the following poem, "Among the Things That Use to Be," written by an African American woman named Willi Coleman.

Use to be
Ya could learn a whole lot of stuff
sitting in them
beauty shop chairs
Use to be
Ya could meet
a whole lot of other women
sittin there
along with hair frying
spit flying
and babies crying
Use to be
you could learn a whole lot about
how to catch up
with yourself

and some other folks
in your household.
Lots more got taken care of
than hair
Cause in our mutual obvious dislike
for nappiness
we came together
under the hot comb
to share
and share
and share
But now we walk
heads high
naps full of pride
with not a backward glance
at some of the beauty which
use to be
Cause with a natural
there is no natural place
for us to congregate
to mull over
our mutual discontent
Beauty shops
could have been
a hell-of-a-place
to ferment
a. . . . . . . .revolution.[4]

This poem, while confirming my own findings in the beauty shop I studied and my feelings while sitting in Miss Ruby's chair, led me to search for a culturally specific understanding of hair and the politics that surround it in writings by African American women. I discovered that the feelings I recalled were present for other African American women as well. For example, bonding is the subject of bell hooks's article "Straightening Our Hair," in which she points out that in spite of the politics of straight versus natural hair, she fondly remembers the Saturday morning ritual of having her hair straightened with her sisters. What she recalls is a time of closeness between her and the women with whom she shared her life.[5] Along similar lines, Andrea Benton Rushing writes that although she taught her daughters to value natural hair, she, a beautician's daughter, recognized that that stance left out what she considered an important part of her daughters' history and culture.[6]

If contemporary writers and poets were interested in discussing the politics of hair straightening in terms of a bonding ritual in which women could come together to touch, nourish, and sustain themselves, whereas others declared their blackness by not straightening their hair, I was left to wonder about the origins of such sentiments. They could not have sprung full blown from a contemporary imagination. Although my initial interests led me forward to the present, the work and figures that I became most interested in were in the past and centered on the social, economic, and cultural politics surrounding hair in the early twentieth century.

What I "discovered" there was a group of African American women, one generation removed from slavery, who began a conscious process of positioning African American women's identity within their communities through advertisements for hair-care products. In the process, these women and their advertisements critiqued class constructions in African American communities, argued for equality in gender relations, and resisted the dominant culture's prevailing ideologies surrounding beauty. All of this took place in relation to hair.

In this book, I examine some of these hair advertisements, taken primarily from African American publications in the late nineteenth and early twentieth century. This advertising, as it relates to the construction of a historical African American female identity, is crucial. In the process, I focus on the changing ideological significance of the look, care, and means of styling hair in African American women's lives.

I used advertisements for support when I confronted my mother with my desire to straighten my hair, and I contend here that African American women in earlier periods would have used advertisements as they struggled to define their relationship to the culture in which they lived. Whereas the majority of beauty advertisements before 1904 were crafted by white-owned companies, after that period, African American women began to market hair and beauty products aimed at other African American women. Because most of these companies were small, the female owners created the advertisements themselves and, as a result, had a hands-on relationship with an emerging discourse on hair that had far-ranging consequences. Roland Marchand has suggested that once advertisements are placed in the same category with many traditional historical documents, it "may be possible to argue that ads actually surpass most other recorded communications as a basis for *plausible inference* about popular attitudes and values."[7] Through advertisements, one may discern culturally acceptable fashions and hairstyles that promise not only the means of achieving beauty but a particularized bodily relation to the dominant culture. As Barbara Welch-Breeder explains, "[advertisements] serve a dual function—on the one hand, they provide models and information which assist the individual in placing his or her experience within a meaningful construction and, on the other hand, they reflect those constructions which are considered meaningful and acceptable within a given culture."[8]

Although the production, selling, and consumption of products in African American beauty culture is a capitalist venture, what is at stake are not only implicit economic relationships but, more importantly, culturally specific strategies and symbols in the daily lives of African American women. This is significant in that only in the past few decades have African American women appeared regularly in roles other than the traditional Jezebel, Mammy, Maid, or Sapphire figure in the mass media of television, films, and videos. Newspapers and magazines, a part of the African American cultural landscape since 1827, when the *Freedman's Journal* first began publication, have, however, always featured advertisements.[9]

To place these advertisements in a broad cultural context, I examine the debates on hair straightening, the marketing image of African American women as both producers and consumers of hair-care products, and larger exchanges on the most expedi-

ent means of achieving "racial progress," class mobility, and
social equality during the Progressive Era (1880–1920).

Whereas hair, and the general problematic of beauty, is a topic
that has appeared often in the writings of white feminist historians and theorists, they generally fail to take into account the
specific differences in meaning and forms of expression that
African American and white women have assigned to it. For
example, Lois Banner's *American Beauty*, a work that claims to
chronicle manifestations of American beauty over two cen-
turies, makes only two references to African American women
in the course of three hundred pages, and then collapses racial
differences between white and African American women. Unfortunately, this is a common problem in mainstream feminist
scholarship, which too often essentializes women and thereby
fails to take into account specificities of the different types of
women constituting American womanhood.[10]

This same pattern may be observed in other works by feminists writing about personal beauty. Susan Brownmiller's chapter titled "Hair," in her book *Femininity*, is exemplary of this
shortcoming. Brownmiller acknowledges the differences in the
nature and texture of "African American" and "white" hair as
well as the specific ways that these differences function in African American and white cultures. Through her readings of
works by two African American women writers, Ntozake
Shange and Toni Morrison, she notes the African American
terms "good" and "bad" hair. However, she brings to this discussion extracultural determinants of the hair types that character-
ize good and bad "white" hair, and leads readers to believe that
African American women only react to external racial pressures
in the styling of their hair. That is, she assumes white women's
reasons for considering their hair to be "good" or "bad" are the
same ones African American women would have.[11] In this
book, I assess more subtle and, I think, more telling and persua-
sive cultural articulations of the functions that hair performs in
the lives and perceptions of African American women.

Forward to the Past: Advertising Hair in African American
Women's History

Since the 1830s, the merchandising, by white-owned companies, of hair-care products specifically designed to straighten
hair have appeared in African American periodicals. However,
just as the products could only promise a caricature of white
standards of beauty, so too the pictures that accompanied the
ads were caricatures of a standard of beauty that was difficult, if
not impossible, for African American women to meet.

The technique that these mail-order hair-straightening products advised was to wash the hair, lay it out flat, and then apply
the hair-straightening solution, using a hot flat iron to iron it in.
Even washed and laid out, the hair of many African American
women was not long enough to iron, and burned scalps were
common. Such damage, if beauty advertisements are to be believed, often caused African American women to suffer from
baldness at an early age. Clearly, these methods were far from
safe. Not only were African American women told by the larger
society that something was lacking in their appearance, but
when they tried to change that appearance and bring it more
into line with what advertisements told them was beautiful,
they further exacerbated the problem.

In public discussions of the societal consequences of hair
straightening, manufacturers of the products urged African
American women to straighten their hair to foster societal acceptance. However, many African Americans, even then, argued that straightened hair amounted to a disavowal of African
ancestry. Within this exchange, hair, or its natural texture, was
discussed as one of the most reliable indicators of racial
heritage.

In a debate that took place during the winter of 1914, an-
thropologist Franz Boas was called on to verify racial heritage.
The headline to an article that appeared in the *New York Age*
reads, "Can Science Tell Negro Blood? Dr. Boas Has Hard

Task."[12] The article states that Boas was called on to decide whether the wife of a prominent Detroit physician was a white woman or a "Negro." Her husband was suing for divorce because he did not believe his wife was a white orphan, as she claimed, but rather the daughter of a full-blooded Negro man and a Colored (half white) matron of a railroad station in Cincinnati.

In the article, the wife, Mrs. Little, is described as a golden-haired blonde with beautiful gray eyes and regular features. After looking at the newspaper's pictures of her, Boas immediately said she was not the daughter of a full-blooded "Negro." In explaining the various methods anthropologists would use to determine whether she had any Negro ancestry, Boas added, "If this woman has any of the characteristics of the Negro race it would be easy to find them. If she has Negro blood in her veins she may have them. One characteristic that is regarded as reliable is *the hair. You can tell by a microscopic examination of a cross section of hair to what race that person belongs*" (italics mine). Although skin color has been seen as a more prominent attribute for such determinations, no product has been invented that consistently changes the pigmentation of the skin (Michael Jackson aside). The hair's texture, however, can be changed, so advertisements for such beauty products had wide-ranging consequences in dominant as well as African American culture and society. In this work, I look at such turn-of-the-century intersections of hair, culture, gender, class, race, and advertisements.

An Overview

During the late nineteenth and early twentieth century, scientists, anthropologists, and laypeople relied on a strict racial hierarchy as the foundation for their beliefs about race, intelligence, and social mobility. In this book I look at the relationship between ideologies of race and beauty conventions and identify the cultural context within which African American women functioned during that period as they created companies that marketed beauty to other African American women. This volume is also aimed at understanding the ways that dominant ideologies surrounding race and beauty were articulated by writers and speakers in African American communities within turn-of-the-century discourses on black pride.

The terms of this discussion were cast into simplistic binary opposites of positive/negative, good/bad images that privileged the first term in light of a white norm. This discussion was further complicated by the class and gender of the participants, who, according to Cornel West, were anxiety-ridden, middle-class black intellectuals (and predominantly male and heterosexual). Grappling with their sense of "double-consciousness," namely, their own crisis of identity, agency, and audience, they were caught "between a quest for White approval and acceptance and an endeavor to overcome the internalized association of Blackness with inferiority."[13]

In coming to understand how African American men portrayed women and looking at the connections they made between gender and the possibility of beauty for African American women, I examine in chapter 2 the ways that African American women's bodies were appropriated and used as a terrain upon which meaning was inscribed and ideologies illustrated. To understand the effects of such practices, I also examine the ways African American women constructed identities for and meanings about their own bodies within advertisements for hair products.

African American women engaged in the production of culture at the level of advertisements "talked back" to dominant culture's undergirding premises about connections between race and the possibility of physical beauty. In addition, their advertisements critiqued African American male as well as middle-class assumptions regarding the rationales for particular beauty regimes such as hair straightening. Because, as Stuart Hall has stated, identity is a production that "is never complete, always in process, and always constituted within, not outside of representation,"[14] their representations of African American women and the ways in which they chose to frame those representations are significant. Indeed, the representation of hair and the discussions of the meaning of African American women's relationship to their hair illustrate the extent to which hair becomes synonymous with politics and the construction of a group identity.

Whereas the women who shaped these advertisements were certainly major forces, they are presented as precursors to Madam C. J. Walker. In chapter 3, I focus on Walker, arguably one of the most influential individuals in visually representing and constructing identities of African American women at the turn of the century. Walker is credited with popularizing the straightening comb. As a result, her advertisements, speeches, and self-authored newspaper articles are a key place to go for understanding what was involved in an early twentieth-century rationale for hair straightening and the meaning of natural hair. She also exemplifies and in some ways defines the relationship between hair, beauty, business, politics, and economic realities during this crucial period.

Walker's desire to "improve" her appearance (especially her hair) may have been a result of feelings of inadequacy in relation to beauty standards set up in the dominant culture's ideological discourses. But it is significant that she chose to locate her desire to change her appearance within an African American community and to position members of that community as her standard. This is meaningful in that intellectual leaders and participants in discourses surrounding black pride argued that white standards and imagery were so pervasive that they could not help but affect the majority of African Americans who came into contact with them. Walker, however, located her standard differently and, in discussing her reasons for desiring to change her appearance, did not call upon whiteness or white standards as a rationale.

Madam C. J. Walker's approach to advertising her products highlighted gender relations and inequalities and challenged hegemonic ideologies about the proper place for African American women in their communities. By focusing on attributes other than those generally connected with "New Negros" or the elite professional class of African Americans committed to defining identities for an African American populace, Walker broadened "acceptable" public representations of working-class African American women by urging them to join her in careers outside of the domestic sphere.

Walker emphasized three basic points—economic self-sufficiency, divine inspiration, and health and beauty concerns. For example, in business meetings and conventions, Walker discussed the ways she had "pulled herself up by the boot-straps" to begin a business and build her own factory. She highlighted her business achievements and the way her business could help African Americans better their economic condition by either selling her products or taking one of her mail-order courses and going into business for themselves. This, she argued, would ameliorate their class position in America.

By contrast, when advertising and speaking to groups of African American women, Walker utilized that same basic message to urge women to gain "real economic freedom" by going into business and freeing themselves from dependence on men and the white community. Implying that real as opposed to fictional economic freedom could be had by women only if they were no longer taken care of by men, Walker shifted the significance of that freedom from broad racial signification to one that spoke specifically to women of a certain class. Walker's arguments, as I discuss in chapter 3, are similar to those my grandmother made regarding straight hair and certain classes of African American women.

Walker utilized slide shows, newspaper articles, and speeches to build an overall story or image of her life. In using that image to make money, she broadly distributed her message about African American women and their relationships to beauty, African American men, ideologies of economic uplift, and the African American "masses." Here, it becomes apparent that she had to work through diametrically opposed positions. Chapter 3 focuses primarily on the contradictions Walker embraced as she defined a relationship between hair and money for many African American women at the turn of the century. It was said in various newspaper articles that at the time of her death, Walker employed 100,000 African American women. Some of these women were sales agents, charged with marketing her products; others were hairdressers who used her method of hair care and her products exclusively. In any case, Walker had a lot to do with hairdressing as a career choice for African American women. As a result, when I sat in Miss Ruby's chair and contemplated a career as a hairdresser, unbeknown to me, I owed a debt to Madam C. J. Walker. Although few households had the income to allow African American women the luxury of staying at home, middle-class African American men urged that women be trained for jobs that could be performed in the home. Walker, however, had very different ideas about where African American women should be and the role of hair in making that possible.

Chapter 4 serves to contextualize African American women's historical relationship with their hair through their relationship to gender roles. Although Walker's advertisements were visual representations of African American women, she was also interested in finding a means of offering insights and views on gender relations, women in business, and the importance of political activity in African American women's lives; she wanted access to a medium that would give her broader possibilities. Although her frequent speaking engagements offered her opportunities to discuss these issues, she was interested in publishing a magazine so that her agents would have a vehicle for self-representation and a forum for speaking about what gender meant to them on a number of levels.

Although there were numerous magazines created, published, and edited by African Americans during the first few decades of the twentieth century, only a handful could boast creative editorial control by African American women. Of these, there were only two—*Half-Century* and *Woman's Voice*—marketed specifically to African American women. The latter, funded by the Walker Company, grew out of Walker's efforts to organize African American women into political groups. Although there is no evidence to suggest that Walker contributed articles or performed editorial duties for *Woman's Voice*, the representations and ideologies exhibited in the magazine, the critiques of gender roles, and the calls for more active participation in business and political spheres duplicate Walker's own positions.

Chapter 5 shows how Walker's interests fit a broader social agenda of self-representation and cultural identity as practiced by a group of African American women and exemplified by *Woman's Voice*'s authors and editors as well as its publisher. Here I argue that this magazine was significant primarily because it addressed the changes in home and family relationships brought about because of African American women's entry into the business sphere. This chapter also looks at the ways a group of hairdressers used their career as an opportunity to discuss the place of gender in African American women's lives.

Chapter 6 discusses the legacy of Madam Walker and looks again at contemporary hair politics from the mid-1940s to the present. The overwhelming concern here is understanding where the legacy of hair politics in the early years of this century has left us. This chapter comes to an position on if and how we are taking the discussion about hair to another level. Toward that end, it discusses hair-care advertisements from the 1940s on and looks at the place of African American hair in contemporary cultural productions.

My efforts throughout this book are aimed at increasing our understanding of the politics of being in an African American woman's body during the Progressive Era and the politics that influenced the choices African American women made when representing themselves, particularly their hair. In the process, I attempt to unravel the tangled meaning of hair in African American women's lives. I think it may most aptly be described as reclaiming and understanding a legacy whose contemporary manifestations we are familiar with but whose origins are unclear or have been covered over.

Although hair and the politics of hair are my main topics, this volume is more than an opportunity to examine one of the body's physical attributes. I discuss the significance of hair in order to discuss the politics of representation as it relates to the construction of an African American female identity and various positions surrounding the meaning of African American women's bodies in a broad social context. Taken as a whole, this work juxtaposes the representation of African American women's bodies with self-representations, heightening our understandings of various social positions and their role in structuring the ideological meanings that undergird our understanding of African American women of both the Progressive Era and today. I hope this book will help us understand how hair came to mean so much and how these understandings are transmitted and communicated in African American communities.

In recent years, scholars have begun to devote their time to the frustrating but rewarding task of reconstructing a history of African American women.[15] As a result, we are beginning to learn some of the particulars of African American women's lives and the politics of the old South from the 1600s to the present. Thanks to work done by Victoria Bynum, Deborah Gray White, Anne Scott, Jacqueline Jones, Paula Giddings, Dorothy Sterling, Elizabeth Fox-Genovese, Darlene Clark Hines, and others, we now know that there were African American women such as Frances Ellen Harper who, during the 1800s and before, spoke out against slavery with the same conviction, eloquence, and force exhibited by such white abolitionists as William Lloyd Garrison.

We now know about such African American women as Ida B. Wells and Mary Church Terrell, who held their own with Frederick Douglass and Henry Highland Garnet, two acknowledged

African American intellectuals of the time. We have also learned much more about the day-to-day realities of life in the plantation South and the power relationships that existed in the North during and after Reconstruction. Much of the work, however, has focused on the ways African American women were defined by the culture in which they lived as opposed to understanding the ways these women struggled to define themselves. That is to say, how did African American women during the first few years of the twentieth century begin to make meaning of their lives and bodies, and how did those meanings manifest themselves culturally? This work attempts to begin the process of answering some of these questions.

2

Beauty, Race, and Black Pride

During the 1850s, an African American woman named Charlotte Forten Grimké wrote the following passage in her journal:

> Have been under-going a thorough self-examination. The result is a mingled feeling of sorrow, shame and self-contempt. Have realized more deeply and bitterly than ever in my life my own ignorance and folly. Not only am I without the gifts of Nature, wit, beauty and talent . . . but I am not even *intelligent.* . . . Hattie Purvis is [however] quite attractive, with such long, light hair, and beautiful blue eyes. She is a sweet gentle creature. . . . I have fallen quite in love with her.[1]

Grimké was free during a time when most African Americans were held as slaves, she was educated in languages and "fine" literature when it was uncommon for African Americans and women to be able to make such claims, and she enjoyed considerable social standing in her hometown of Philadelphia. In addition, others who came into contact with her had only the highest praise for her beauty, refinement, and intellect.

The celebrated poet, abolitionist, and editor John Greenleaf Whittier described Grimké as "a young lady of exquisite refinement, quiet culture and ladylike and engaging manners, and personal appearance. She is one of the most gifted representatives of her class" (32). This sentiment was echoed by a writer for the *Salem Register,* who said, "She presented in her own mental endowments and propriety of demeanor an honorable vindication of the claims of her race to the rights of mental culture and the privileges of humanity" (33).

Her advantages and the favorable impression she made on others make it difficult to comprehend why Grimké came to see herself as both ignorant and unattractive. In trying to understand her feelings about beauty, we need a contextualization of beauty discourses of the period. During the antebellum era, what did popular culture tell African American women such as Grimké about their relationship to beauty, and what was the role hair played in this discussion?

As early as the 1830s, the merchandising of hair-care products was common in African American periodicals published in the North. Also, beauty parlors operated by and for African American women were early entrepreneurial ventures among northern free women. Cecilia Remond Putnam, Marchita Remond, and Caroline Remond Putnam (the three sisters of abolitionist lecturer Sarah Parker Remond) owned the fashionable Ladies Hair Work Salon in Salem, Massachusetts. They also owned the largest wig factory in the state, and Mrs. Putnam's Medicated Hair Tonic was sold widely as an antidote to hair loss, which seems to have been a common problem among African American women.

Ascertaining the ideals and practices of female beauty in slave communities, however, involves far more speculation. We surmise that influences would be of a more personal variety because of the lack of newspapers and magazines in slave communities and the high rate of illiteracy among slaves. If any free women of color lived in the area, perhaps they were looked up to, or perhaps house slaves whom the master held in particularly high esteem were held in high regard.

Also, of course, the white mistress may have served as a powerful example of the white standard of beauty. As Elizabeth Fox-Genovese points out, in terms of the importance placed on clothes, slave women who worked in the house "shared slaveholding women's appreciation of dress as the badge of class or quality."[2] It is also possible that such values were communicated to the more general slave population.

Because female slaves probably looked to the values and materials of the white mistress with regard to clothing, they may have done the same with hair, although their practices would have differed. Portraits of slave women show them wearing bandannas covering their hair, as most agricultural and domestic workers did. Fox-Genovese quotes a former slave in Texas, Amos Lincoln, as saying, "the gals dressed up on Sunday. All week they wear they hair all roll up with cotton. . . . Sunday come they com' the hair out fine. No grease on it. They want it naturally curly" (216). What Lincoln is describing is a natural precursor to the contemporary practice of African American women rolling their hair and setting it under a dryer. Working in the sun, they tied a bandanna on the head to lessen the chance of heat stroke and to keep the hair cleaner than if it were exposed to the elements. The tightly wrapped head rag absorbed perspiration and "trained" hair growth.

Whereas slave women may have had to rely on such practices to achieve a beauty standard, Grimké, a well-educated, free northern woman, would not have had to go to such lengths. Advertisements for beauty products would have told her what was considered beautiful and how to achieve the desired look. Indeed, Grimké's harsh self-assessment may be explained by looking closely at the ways she equated morphological features with character. She believed that "Nature" deemed it impossible for her to possess characteristics of "wit, beauty and talent," which were thought to be inherent in "true women" of the day.

As a result, Grimké had feelings of "sorrow, shame and contempt" for herself. However, she loved Hattie Purvis. Indeed, when juxtaposing her own qualities with those of Purvis, Grimké fairly sings the praises of her counterpart, based solely on the latter's physical characteristics—hair texture, hair length, and eye color. She then draws a connection between these characteristics and character. Purvis is "sweet and gentle." Grimké is unpleasant and unattractive. These beliefs would have been supported by the advertisements for beauty products marketed at that time.

Driven primarily by popular ideas about race, early mail-order advertisements discuss African Americans as "suffering" from an African heritage and searching for the "cure" that whiteness can offer. Within these advertising discourses, racial ideologies are written primarily onto the bodies (skin and hair) of African American women.

Racial Ideologies and Early Beauty Advertisements

It appears that late nineteenth- and early twentieth-century beauty companies depended on the commonly held belief of a racial hierarchy and maintained it in their advertisements, even those aimed at an African American audience.[3] Advertisements for skin lighteners and hair straighteners marketed by white companies suggest to blacks that only through changing physical features will persons of African descent be afforded class mobility within African American communities and social acceptance by the dominant culture. With the exception of wig manufacturers, no other companies advertised for products aimed at enhancing African American beauty. Whereas in the dominant press, companies advertised everything from cures for neurasthenia to girdles and other types of garments, as well as different lotions and ointments aimed at making skin look softer and more youthful, in the black press, African American women were bombarded solely with products that promised to lighten the skin and straighten the hair.

Four products advertised regularly between 1866 and 1905 were Black Skin Remover, Black and White Ointment, Ozonized Ox Marrow, and Curl-I-Cure: A Cure for Curls. The first two were skin lighteners, and the latter two claimed to straighten African American hair. The advertisements argue for the desirability of changing physical manifestations of "classic" African features by juxtaposing the characteristics of Caucasians and Africans to highlight the advantages of disavowing the physical manifestations of an African ancestry. Although many of the products make claims about their usefulness for African American men, they all utilize images of African American women in their advertisements.

For example, the advertisement for Black Skin Remover and Hair Straightener features "before" and "after" drawings of a woman (fig. 1). The "before" drawing is an outline inked in so dark that one cannot make out the woman's features. However, her forehead slopes forward sharply, and her nose is broad and short. Her hair is short, curly, and looks uncombed. The "after" drawing shows the change that will occur once the product is used. The woman's hair has become long and straight and is neatly styled. Her skin is white and her forehead no longer slopes forward as drastically. Her nose has become long and aquiline. Not only has her skin color and hair texture changed, but so has her bone structure.

The two figures face each other and appear to be looking into each other's eyes. Because the dark figure's eyes are obscured by her black skin, she can only look out into darkness and cannot actually see how unattractive she is or the white woman she could become. The white figure, however, can look back at the African American woman she used to be. Along with her white skin, she has now gained the privilege of sight. It is possible to envision the dark figure as the self Charlotte Forten Grimké loathed and the white figure as Hattie Purvis, whom she loved. The positioning of these two figures speaks to the racial ideologies that undergird the advertisement. The removal of "black skin" allows for a forward movement toward civiliza-

A Wonderful Face Bleach.

AND HAIR STRAIGHTENER.

Fig. 1. Black skin bleach and hair straightener.

tion, as illustrated by the straight, neatly combed hair. The presence of black skin marks a person as primitive, unclean, and ignorant. After using the product, the image has become a "beauty," as opposed to the "beast" she once was. Although the product's name suggests that it is only skin color that is at issue, the images foreground the physical changes that must necessarily follow to reposition oneself in the racial hierarchy.

This advertisement also speaks to the ways that ideologies of gender and race interacted to circumscribe the identities of African American women. Before using the product, the figure is neither male nor female but a faceless blob. The presence of blackness precludes gender identification as well as the possibility of femininity for African American women. There is no doubt that the "before" drawing represents the least desirable of the two figures. The body of the African American woman is solely constructed in opposition to the figure of the white woman, and African American women among the advertisement's readership are asked to think of their bodies as imperfect. The beauty standard here is not merely proximity to whiteness but whiteness itself: "A peach-like complexion obtained if used as directed. Will turn the skin of a black or brown person four or five shades lighter, and a mulatto person perfectly white. In forty-eight hours a shade or two will be noticeable. It does not turn the skin to spots but bleaches out white, the skin remaining beautiful without continual use" (*St. Louis Palladium*, 1901). Here the manufacturers promise that members of the African American community can attain skin that is not just white but "perfectly" white. In speaking to what they see as variations in skin tone within the African American community, they point out that their products have something to offer everyone, from the darkest to the lightest members. While the product does not claim to make a dark-skinned person white, it will lighten her, and a fair-skinned or mulatto person can rid her skin of all traces of an African heritage.

Because these manufacturers speak of black skin in the same context as an imperfection that can be fixed, it is positioned as a

*dis*ease or blemish. The advertising copy continues: "Will re-
move wrinkles, freckles, dark spots, pimples or bumps or black
heads. . . . Small pox pits and liver spots removed. . . . When
you get the color you wish, stop using the product." As a result,
dark skin is discussed in opposition to the ease of one's life once
it is removed. The cure is fast. In only forty-eight hours, one
should see a difference. Also, the user is in control of the process. When she has reached the desired color, she may choose to
stop. In this way, the manufacturers market beauty based on
whiteness, and by extension, superiority in a thinly disguised
rhetoric of free will and control.

This sentiment is echoed in an ad for Black and White Ointment, but the manufacturer makes explicit the connection between dark skin and slavery as well as diminished chances for
success in American society. The "after" lithograph here has
been replaced by a photograph of a fair-skinned African American woman, and the advertising copy commands readers to
"Lighten Your Dark Skin": "Race men and women protect your
future. . . . Be Attractive. Throw off the chains that have held
you back from prosperity and happiness that rightly belong to
you. Apply Black and White Ointment (for white or colored
folks) as directed on package. . . . Be the envy of everybody"
(*New York Age*, 1919). The manufacturer uses direct address to
remind those of African descent that their color was responsible
for an enslaved condition less than a generation ago. By admon-
ishing African American women to "protect your future," they
raise the specter of a return to slavery for those whose color
remains dark. By arguing that "prosperity" and "happiness"
rightly belong to them, the advertisement suggests that it is skin
color alone that keeps them from attaining these rewards, and
that, the manufacturer promises, may be changed by purchasing the product.

This advertisement also includes a short testimonial from an
African American woman who claims to have been helped by
using this product. In keeping with the strategy of direct address used by the manufacturer, Viola Steele addresses the

anonymous reader as "dear friends." She then goes on to say that she was worried by freckles, blackheads, and sunburn and that the product has bleached her skin. Whereas the headline for the advertisement indicates that one should use the product to lighten dark skin, the spokeswoman does not mention that as the reason she purchased the product. She merely wanted to rid herself of a few freckles and blackheads. This statement, however, is not emphasized in the advertisement. What is highlighted is the headline and the large photograph of a light-skinned African American woman commanding others to lighten their skin. While her inclusion could undermine the racial ideology that undergirds the advertisement, she is reinscribed within the context of that ideology. Her body is positioned as an object.

Also interesting are the references to the product's use by white as well as African American clients. This strategy may have been aimed at light-skinned African Americans who could "pass" for white or at those of European descent whose dark skin also identified and circumscribed their class and social status. For African Americans, however, skin color functioned as a marker of a racial identity, which often was spoken of as simply inferior. In marketing products that were said to lessen the shame of such a marker, beauty manufacturers in the nineteenth century targeted skin color and hair texture—the two characteristics African Americans had to change if they expected to fit into American society.

By the turn of the century, ads for Ozonized Ox Marrow were an advertising staple in the *St. Louis Palladium* as well as in a majority of other African American newspapers (fig. 2). The advertisement features a bold headline stating "Wonderful Discovery, Curly Hair Made Straight By Original Ozonized Ox Marrow" and a sketch of an African American woman said to be "taken from life." In the "before" drawing, the woman's hair is shown almost standing on end, whereas the "after" drawing portrays the hair as neatly combed and styled. The advertising copy proclaims, "This wonderful hair pomade is the only safe

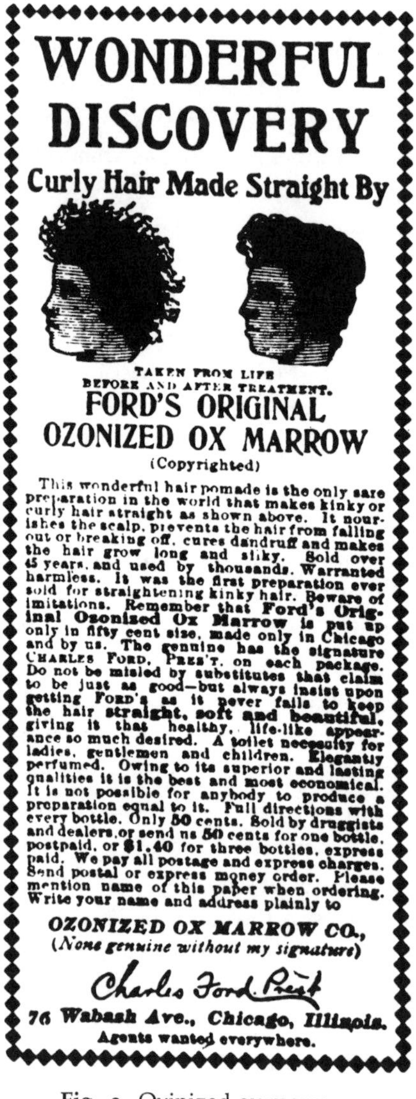

Fig. 2. Oxinized ox marrow.

preparation in the world that makes kinky or curly hair straight as shown above. . . . A toilet necessity for ladies, gentlemen and children" (*St. Louis Palladium*, 1903). One could easily assume that natural hair cannot be combed, because these advertisements never portray curly hair as combed or styled in the least. In addition, this ad makes an explicit connection between the product and class status by using words such as "ladies" and "gentlemen." Not for use by just anyone, rather, this product is a necessity for those who wish to raise themselves above the common masses. As a result, it articulates a connection between physical features and class mobility.

Such sentiments are also evident in the advertisement for Curl-I-Cure: A Cure For Curls (fig. 3): "You owe it to yourself, as well as to others who are interested in you, to make yourself as attractive as possible. Attractiveness will contribute much to your success—both socially and commercially. Positively nothing detracts so much from your appearance as short, matted un-attractive curly hair" (*St. Louis Palladium*, 1905). This manufacturer believes that women should be concerned with how their appearance affects those who must look at them. It is unfair, the advertisement implies, to force members of society to look at an African American woman's body whose African ancestry she has not disavowed. Moreover, it is not acceptable. An acceptable appearance means ridding oneself of "short, matted un-attractive curly hair" and replacing it with hair that is long, silky, and straight. Acceptability means ridding one's self of natural hair. The lithograph of the African American woman is said to have been "Taken From Life After Two Weeks' Use." The woman looks back over her shoulder at a past we cannot know. However, we do know that if the rhetoric in the advertisement is correct, her future will contain both social and commercial success. The advertisement continues, "If you have not individuality you enjoy no advantages. There is one way and only one way in which you can overcome this great handicap." The manufacturer asserts that advancement may be had only by changing the hair's texture. Not education, wealth, social position,

Fig. 3. Curl-I-Cure.

manners, morals, or breeding will be effective. African American women's bodies are again positioned as handicapped or imperfect and incapable of representing a standard of beauty constructed outside of dominant ideologies surrounding race.

Another company urges its readers to "Have soft, straight hair like the photograph below." It continues: "Race men and women may easily have straight, soft, long hair by simply applying Plough's Hair Dressing and in a short time all your kinky, snarly, ugly, curly hair becomes soft, silky, smooth, straight, long and easily handled, brushed or combed" (*New York Age*, 1910). Looking at the language used to describe African Americans, we see there is nothing positive these manufacturers consider worthy of praising. Black skin is to be "removed" and replaced with beautiful skin either shades lighter or white. Dark skin is connected to a dark past of roughly a generation ago, and a brighter future depends on brighter or lighter skin tone.

The advertising copy for hair straighteners is equally disparaging. Before treatment, African American hair is referred to as kinky, snarly, ugly, and curly. The language shapes or constructs that community as forever trapped by its circumstances and imprisoned by its features. Because all of these advertisements derive their significance from the racial ideologies that undergird them, the meaning of African American women's bodies pictured in the advertisements is solely articulated within that construct. It is at the level of their bodies that the rational for changing or disavowing an African ancestry is articulated.

Although there were undoubtedly many African Americans who shared these advertisers and Grimké's views regarding African American physical inferiority, there were also those who critiqued such connections and argued for a standard of beauty that was located in African physiology. Indeed, the issue of beauty standards and of their effects on African Americans was an integral part of nineteenth-century "Black Pride" discourses that linked "beauty" to a call for the production of imagery that would combat the damaging representations in dominant culture.

For example, writing in the March 11, 1853, *Frederick Douglass' Paper*, William J. Wilson voiced these concerns in an editorial titled "White is Beautiful": "We despise, we almost hate ourselves, and all that favors us. Well we scoff at black skins and woolly heads, since every model set before us for admiration has a pallid face and flaxen head." Although Wilson's reference to "pallid faces" and "flaxen heads" may refer either to African Americans with white ancestry, and therefore with a higher class status, or to images of European Americans, his illustration helps elucidate the feelings Grimké probably shared with many African American women.

Wilson's comments prefigured by a century Kenneth Clark's doll study that was crucial to the outcome of the 1954 *Brown v. the Board of Education of Topeka, Kansas* Supreme Court decision on school desegregation. Wilson suggests that the way to change young girls' fear of dark skin is for African Americans to begin to participate in particular acts of cultural production:

> Every one of your readers knows that a black girl would as soon fondle an imp as a black doll—such is the force of this species of education upon her. I remember once having introduced one among a company of twenty colored girls, and if it had been a spirit, the effect could not have been more wonderful. Such scampering and screaming can better be imagined than told. No, no; we must begin to tell our own story, write our own lecture, paint our own picture, chisel our own bust, acknowledge and love our own peculiarities.

He urges African Americans to "write, paint, and sculpt" in a way that will highlight what he terms the "peculiarities" or differences between African Americans and European Americans.

What is unspoken in Wilson's argument is the need for those images produced by African Americans to be taken up and understood in a way that mediates the power of dominant discourses. However, he argues implicitly that only acts of cultural production by the middle classes will accomplish this task. But what of those who cannot write or sculpt? What of the majority of African Americans who, during that period, were still bound as slaves and usually denied the luxury of learning to read and write let alone paint and sculpt? Thus Wilson speaks to class distinctions in African American communities by arguing that changes in attitudes among all African Americans will occur when the middle and upper classes begin to engage in formal acts of cultural production.

Whereas Wilson was concerned with the psychological effects of internalized oppression and the need for a more "authentic" representation of the self, Martin Freeman decries the lengths to which African Americans would go to approximate Anglo-Saxon standards of personal beauty. In an April 1859 article in the *Anglo-African Magazine,* Freeman offers a vivid description of hairstyling practices and a stern critique of those who imitated European standards of beauty:

> The child is taught directly or indirectly that he or she is pretty, just in proportion as the features approximate the Anglo-Saxon standard. Hence flat noses must be pinched up. Kinky hair must be subjected to a straightening process—oiled, and pulled, twisted up, tied down, sleeked over and pressed under, or cut off so short that it can't curl, sometimes the natural hair is shaved off and its place supplied by a straight wig. Thick lips are puckered up and drawn in. Beautiful black and brown faces by the application of rouge and lily white powder are made to assume unnatural tints, like the livid hue of painted corpses.[4]

Like Wilson, Freeman is disturbed by the ways physical features that speak to an African heritage are perceived as inherently unattractive by African Americans, but he locates the responsibility for this perception firmly within individual African American homes. He is concerned with the socialization process of young children, who cannot hope to find African features desirable because parents and other adults spend considerable time and effort attempting to change the offending features. Freeman, however, appears interested only in free African Americans, since it is hard to imagine slave women, particularly those who worked in the fields, parading around in "straight wigs" with rouge and powder on their faces.

Freeman ends his editorial by asserting, "Now all this is foolish, perhaps wicked, but under the circumstances it is very natural." His use of the word "natural" refers pointedly to the normalization of ideologies of race, which he understands to be the cause of the behavior he is critiquing. Given the ways that constructions of race during the late nineteenth and early twentieth century posited relationships between physical characteristics and intelligence, potential for civilized behavior, and indeed in some instances, humanity, it is not surprising that Grimké held the beliefs she did.

For example, in his 1848 book, *Natural History of the Human Species,* Charles Hamilton Smith writes that "the typical woolly haired races have never discovered an alphabet, framed a grammatical language, nor made the least step in science or art."[5] Smith's "woolly haired race" is a metaphor for African physical traits, which serve as prima facie evidence of racial difference as mental "lack" and as a justification for slavery and racial discrimination. Smith, considered a pioneer of racial typology in Britain, puts forth his views regarding the three typical "stocks" of mankind—the bearded Caucasian, the beardless Mongolian, and the woolly haired Negro—and the role of physical features in placing each on a racial hierarchy.[6]

His work includes a chart that positions the "wooly haired" at the base of a triangular hierarchy he has set up. Caucasians are located at the apex. Smith suggests that the Caucasian was a veritable paragon, the only one to have "produced examples of free and popular institutions . . . ascended to the skies, descended into the deep, and mastered the powers of lightening. . . . He has instituted all the great religious systems in the world, and to his stock has been vouchsafed the glory and the conditions of revelation" (50). The Negro, however, received a lowly place in this racial hierarchy, due mainly to the small brain found in those with dark skin and woolly hair.

In supporting this theory of differing brain sizes, Smith claims that in the West Indies, even the smallest of British army caps issued to black troops proved too big and required padding an inch and a half in thickness to make them fit. However, he points out, the caps fit even noncommissioned officers who were of European descent. He goes on to make an observation that surely must have alarmed any whites who had been nursed as children by slave women when he states that white infants fed on the milk of "Negros" suffered in both appearance and temperament. Smith concludes his work by asserting that any civilized behavior or progress on the part of the "wooly heads" could only be attributed to their contact with those of European descent.

Smith's work was published before Darwin's *Descent of Man* (1871), a volume that signaled a movement among anthropologists and ethnologists away from theories of race that posited polygenists' notions of creation and toward those of the monogenists. However, the racial hierarchy remained in place. The argument then became that, although nonwhites were not created inferior, they were capable of evolving only to a certain level. As George Stocking, Jr., argues in *Race, Culture, and Evolution*, "Darwinian evolution, evolutionary ethnology and polygenist notions interacted [at the turn of the century] to support a racial hierarchy in which large-brained white men, and only large-brained white men, the highest products of superiority, were fully civilized."[7]

It was at the level of the body that such ideologies could be and were played out. Not only was skin color positioned as indicative of intelligence and civilization, but hair texture and facial features were also highlighted as speaking to one's position in the hierarchy of humanity. These racial theories constructed those of African descent as dark-skinned, wooly headed, small-brained primitives who did not have the reasoning capacity to better their place in the racial hierarchy without some direct help and intervention from Europeans. White-owned companies marketing beauty during that time seemed to suggest that the first step was straightening African American hair.

Given these views, it is understandable that African American women as well as men were affected by and concerned with discussing the desirability of maintaining African features and the way those features, particularly "wooly heads," spoke to a pride in African ancestry. It is also understandable that, in attempting to challenge these constructions of African ancestry,

African Americans began to address their communities about the necessity of producing images that contradicted the dominant culture's representations. These same concerns surrounding beauty and race and the place of hair in perceptions of personal beauty were articulated in the early decades of the twentieth century. However, if in the nineteenth century the meaning of racial differences was described in terms of African Americans' relationship to their hair, the significance of hair and its relationship to gender and class within those same communities are the primary focus of the discussion in the early twentieth century. That is, hair becomes a site of African American women's struggle to define their identity and their relationship with men and the middle classes.

Beauty Discourses: The Early Twentieth Century

During the late 1800s, the issue of beauty was discussed most often by middle-class men, so it was primarily a middle-class male voice that constructed public identities for all African Americans. Although there were women who contributed articles and editorials to various African American newspapers and periodicals as well as women who edited publications, they were mainly concerned with discussing the relationship of women to political issues or gender and racial inequalities within their communities. This began to change in the early decades of the twentieth century, as more women, in their writings and speeches, began to address issues of representation, beauty, and the cultural production of images. Even here, however, the perspective most often voiced came from the middle classes.

Nannie H. Burroughs urged African American women to be more concerned with social uplift activities as opposed to white beauty standards: "What does this wholesale bleaching of faces and straightening of hair indicate? It simply means that women who practice it wish that they had white faces and straight hair."[8] Yet she was particularly concerned with issues of beauty and beauty representation. Burroughs, who founded the National Training School for Girls and Women to prepare women for jobs in domestic service (for which she came to be known as the female Booker T. Washington), believed that health and beauty issues were central to this preparation. In a practice unique to Burroughs's school, each morning at six o'clock students were inspected for personal cleanliness and neatness. They were ranked by such factors as body odor, hair, and clothing. A woman could not complete a course of study at Burroughs's school if she did not pass these morning "tests."[9]

Burroughs's concerns were echoed in a February 1920 editorial, titled "Betrayers of the Race," published in *Half-Century Magazine*. In the editorial, an unidentified writer bemoans the sixty advertisements for hair-straightening and skin-lightening solutions published in a single edition of an unnamed African American newspaper. The author calls these companies "fake white concerns who know little or nothing about chemistry and whose owners grow rich and retire to large dwellings all the while laughing at the gullibility of African Americans." This particular magazine's editor-in-chief and associate editor were African American women, which perhaps explains why, instead of simply decrying the use of such products, the editorial goes on to suggest that because fashion dictates some styles as more desirable than others, one can argue that women who use hair-straightening products are merely following fashion. The writer suggests that African American women use these products

> in the same spirit that they wear some of the most ridiculous Paris Fashions—just because the leaders of fashion say it is the proper thing to do. Thousands of white women have their hair straightened because it is quite impossible to "do up" any but the straightest of hair in some of the most approved styles. Colored women have their hair straightened for the same reason. . . . Most white women feel that they would rather be dead than out of style and in that respect their darker sisters do not differ from them one iota.

Although not urging the use of hair straighteners and skin lighteners, the writer offers an alternative reading of that process.
Her concern seems not to lie so much with the political significance of straightening one's hair or lightening one's skin as with
the willingness of African American periodicals to run advertisements that promote such products.

Whereas advertising in African American periodicals before
1906 was dominated by such products as Black Skin Remover
and Curl-I-Cure: A Cure For Curls, numerous companies
owned and operated by African American women began to
advertise in the same newspapers sometime between 1906 and
1919. These advertisements challenged dominant ideologies
and constructions of African American women. By using rhetorical strategies from within African American culture, these
women contested the popular construction of African American women as "other" and addressed them in ways that indicated kinship and acceptance. In the process, they shifted the
significance of African American women's bodies in advertising discourses from concerns with the dominant culture's ideologies of beauty, upward mobility, and social acceptance and
toward concerns with health, versatility of styling, hair length,
and economic well-being. In the process, they recontextualized
the meaning of hair in African American communities and impacted the portrayal of their identities within African American
mass culture.

African American Women: Advertising Beauty

The construction of African American women found in advertisements produced by other African American women does
not suggest a relationship between skin color, hair texture, and
inferiority. Nor do the advertisements propose the necessity for
proficiency in the arts or a cultural realm as a prerequisite for
their product's use. Most often, the manufacturers appear in the
advertisements and tell women that they should be striving for
healthy hair. By using their own bodies as marketing tools, these

early entrepreneurs reconfigured the popular image of African American women as large boned and dark skinned. Also, they often speak specifically about their backgrounds as domestics and laundresses to position their class background.

Many of their advertisements utilized testimonials as well as "before" and "after" self-portraits. Although no evidence suggests that any of these companies advertised widely or for extensive periods of time, the ads constituted a continuing discourse on the politics of constructing an African American female identity. For example, Madam T. D. Perkins's advertisement for her hairdressing services proclaimed her a "Scientific Scalp Specialist." She tells readers, "No matter how dark your skin is," her treatment will "cultivate, beautify and grow a persons hair, so long as there is no physical ailment which will prevent it."

Here Perkins acknowledges racial ideologies that position the presence of dark skin as a disease or at least as an impediment for any type of positive change. However, she repositions this doctrine to reassure those who have doubts about their ability to grow hair. Indeed, by asserting that her product will be successful as long as there is no physical ailment that prevents hair growth, she affectively dislodges the primacy of racial ideologies that articulate African American women's bodies as "lack" and critiques advertisements that utilize this type of reasoning. As a result, she challenges dominant ideologies of race and their connection to conventions of gender and beauty.

The ad includes photographs of the back and front of Perkins's head, with the back shot emphasizing the length of her hair. Underneath this insert is yet another photograph of Madam Perkins, but this time we see her before she began to grow her hair. Here Perkins reworks the concept of "before" and "after." Although she utilizes images of her body both before and after the treatment, she retains the markers of her African ancestry. Unlike those advertisements that promised to fundamentally change the lives as well as the facial structure of African American women, Perkins merely promises to grow hair. Between the first inset and the second is a bold headline: "Women, Stop, Wait, Listen, Read!" and a Bible verse states, "If a Woman have long hair, it is a Glory to Her: 1 Cor 11–15." We are then treated to a two-column story telling us that her hair is her best advertisement and that she is the only manufacturer who can show the true length of her hair before she started using her own preparations. Like earlier advertisements, Perkins uses direct address to speak to the desirability of utilizing her product. However, she does not command African American women to change their bodies to foster social acceptance; she merely asks them to purchase her product. By locating the rationale for her product's use within the context of Scripture, she evokes a form of testifying or bearing witness that is familiar to members of African American communities.

In African American churches, to testify, or bear witness, is to reaffirm one's belief that God and Christian living bring joy. In a testimonial, which usually takes place before or at the beginning of a church service, the speaker asks to be recognized by the church community and then stands up and delivers a monologue addressing all of the rewards he or she has received from God. Perkins uses this basic structure in her advertisement. She asks women readers to "Stop and Listen" to what she has to say. She "stands" to be identified by including a photograph of herself. She then invokes God's name by quoting Scripture and goes on to testify to the product's efficacy. Testimony is the "call" portion of call and response, which is integral to services in African American churches. The "response" would be the purchase and use of her product.

Thus, Perkins's ad combines a number of techniques. She appeals to science as well as to religion and testimony. She also attempts to position her lack of national exposure and agents as a plus by saying that, as a result, her product is more exclusive than products manufactured by her competition. Nowhere, however, does she mention that long hair will somehow bring prosperity or increase chances for acceptance in American society, nor does she discuss African American women as if their characteristics were inherently undesirable. As a result, Perkins constructs an identity and image of beauty for African American women firmly located within the context of African American culture. African American women's bodies are positioned within that community, and the possibility for a beauty standard not undergirded by unfavorable ideologies of race is established.

During this time, many African American women began to manufacture and market similar beauty products, and advertisements for these different hair treatment systems began to spring up in African American newspapers. Advertisements for Lepra S. Smith's preparations show photographs of three different women who either graduated from her studio or are her clients. There is also a letter testifying to Madam Smith's knowledge about growing hair. Madam Newell, on the other hand, offered $100 to anyone proving that her product did not grow hair when used as directed. She added, "Now don't you be satisfied with simply having your hair made to look beautiful, but grasp for all there is in the Crowning Glory of Woman— and let her grow yours."

What is significant here is that the identities of African American women were rarely if ever constructed as somehow lacking what was necessary to prosper in American society; instead, in these ads the focus was on health as well as on various biblical references to "hair as a woman's crown and glory." Other ads urged African American women to become hairdressers and earn money for themselves. Madam J. Nelson's advertisement (fig. 4) told readers they need not "struggle along in uncongenial employment with long hours and short pay. Educate yourself to do work that has little competition; isn't it better to spend a half-hour daily and qualify yourself to do work that everyone else cannot do. The fields are large."

I do not go so far as to suggest that all African American women advertising beauty products during this time were intent on dislodging or contesting the primacy of white constructions of femininity and/or beauty. Neither do I believe that they

Women, Girls, Earn Money

My Free Book Tells How.

LEARN TO GROW HAIR

Don't struggle along in un-congenial employment with long hours and short pay. Educate yourself to do work that has little competition; isn't it better to spend a half-hour daily and qualify yourself to do work that everyone else cannot do. The fields are large.

ELOSO HAIR GROWER
50 Cents Per Box
Are seldom equaled and never excelled

Instructions by mail or in person. Diplomas to graduates. Agents wanted everywhere; don't delay, write today.
A penny will do it.

MME. J. NELSON
ELOSO HAIR GROWER
Manufactured Only By
President of Eloso College Co., 21 S. Compton Avenue, St. Louis, Mo.

Fig. 4. Earn money.

sought to use advertising techniques that employed rhetorical strategies from within African American communities to address their audience. Indeed, there were some, such as Madam Lydia Gardner, who used their bodies to market lip reduction techniques and others who sang the praises of straight hair and urged African American women to purchase their products to lighten their skin.

However, these companies were in the minority. The vast majority were owned by women like Madam M. B. Jackson, who chanted, "If you have good hair, care for it. If you have a diseased scalp, treat it. If you have little or no hair—it's your own fault and a good reason for quick action." This particular advertisement ended by telling readers that her method could be used "with or without straightening the hair" (fig. 5). Hair straightening and threats of inferiority were not the primary

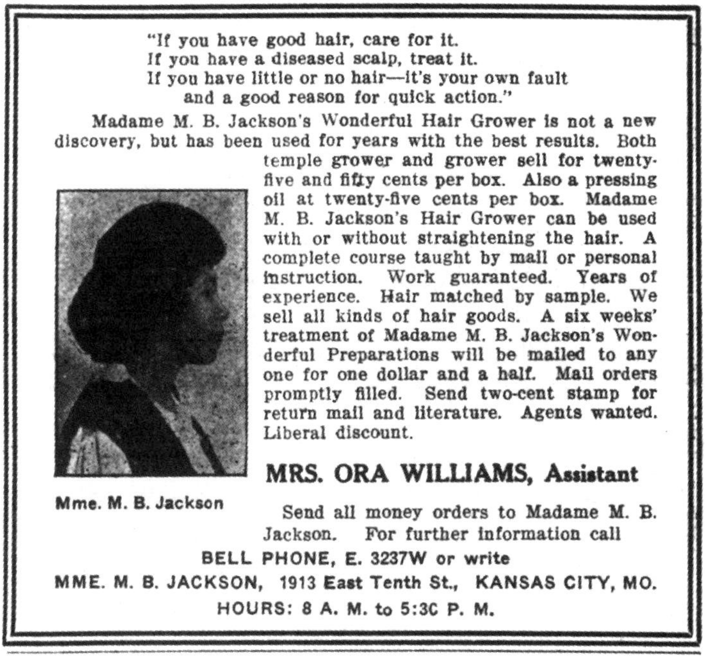

"If you have good hair, care for it.
If you have a diseased scalp, treat it.
If you have little or no hair—it's your own fault
and a good reason for quick action."

Madame M. B. Jackson's Wonderful Hair Grower is not a new discovery, but has been used for years with the best results. Both temple grower and grower sell for twenty-five and fifty cents per box. Also a pressing oil at twenty-five cents per box. Madame M. B. Jackson's Hair Grower can be used with or without straightening the hair. A complete course taught by mail or personal instruction. Work guaranteed. Years of experience. Hair matched by sample. We sell all kinds of hair goods. A six weeks' treatment of Madame M. B. Jackson's Wonderful Preparations will be mailed to any one for one dollar and a half. Mail orders promptly filled. Send two-cent stamp for return mail and literature. Agents wanted. Liberal discount.

MRS. ORA WILLIAMS, Assistant

Mme. M. B. Jackson

Send all money orders to Madame M. B. Jackson. For further information call

BELL PHONE, E. 3237W or write

MME. M. B. JACKSON, 1913 East Tenth St., KANSAS CITY, MO.

HOURS: 8 A. M. to 5:3C P. M.

Fig. 5. Mme. M. B. Jackson.

basis on which these women argued for use of their products. By and large, they attempted to provide a beauty regime for African American women that would allow them to fashion and meet their own ideals as well as create career opportunities for themselves.

While African American intellectuals were either downplaying the importance of outward physical beauty or raging at those who imitated white beauty, agents for hair-straightening systems were actually going door to door to sell these products. Often, agents were members of the community in which they were selling and served as images of African American female beauty. Employing the women who actually used the product to sell door to door was perhaps the most effective marketing tool; they demonstrated visually, and more effectively than a newspaper advertisement, that a particular product really worked. If the product proved unsatisfactory, someone was available who

could be held accountable. These women offered not only images of African American beauty but promoted feelings of trust
of the product. One of the trendsetters for this type of marketing
was Madam Annie Turbo Pope Malone.

Malone advertised a hair grower that she claimed was one of
the "best on the market." During 1908 and 1909, Malone's advertisements generally consisted of the logo for her product;
after 1909, they showed a line drawing of the building in which
she manufactured her preparations. This strategy was quite
different from the methods used by other manufacturers. The
image of the building signifies at several levels. It stands for the
property she was able to purchase as a result of her product's
success. It also signals a certain amount of stability and perma-
nence for the company. By 1910, Malone was advertising in
newspapers from Missouri to Florida. One ad, which ran for
almost a year, includes a profile photo of her and a Mrs. L. L.
Roberts. The advertising copy says, "We grew our hair, now let
us grow yours with Poro" (*St. Louis Palladium,* 1907). Malone's
hair is pictured as four or five inches past her shoulders, and
Mrs. Roberts's hair reaches close to her waist. The caption under
each of the photographs states that four years ago, their hair
was considerably shorter.

Although the company was owned by Malone and no records
indicate that Mrs. Roberts was connected with creating the
product, the headline uses the words "we" and "us." This strategy highlights the fact that the company is owned and operated
by an African American woman and asks, as opposed to commands, that they be given an opportunity to show how well
their product works. This advertisement speaks to African
American women as equals and from a position of familiarity
and kinship.

What is clearly missing from this advertisement is any reference to wanting to grow long hair in an effort to foster class
mobility or societal acceptance. There are no references to
"ugly," "kinky" hair or to the need to change one's hair to fit into
American society; the focus is solely on what the product will

do. Certainly it is possible that those claims did not need to be stated because they were so well known, but it is equally possible that this manufacturer knew that African American women had different reasons for wanting to care for their hair. For example, women who worked and sweated all day would have had to find a convenient means of styling their hair. For African American women with curly hair that would have dried out easily, combing and styling could have been quite a chore. In any case, African American women flocked to use the products that Malone and her colleagues manufactured.

African American women who advertised beauty products produced cultural images that served to re-present the bodies of other women whose race they shared. In the process, they articulated standards of beauty that were not predicated upon unfavorable racial ideologies that structured and undergirded discourses from competing advertising concerns. They drew upon culturally discrete symbols and practices within African American communities and placed African American women's bodies within the context of religious doctrine, which dictated that a woman should strive to have long hair. They also argued that hairdressing was a career choice African American women could ill afford to overlook.

African American women cosmetic manufacturers used a counterhegemonic discourse to critique ideologies of gender, race, and class in the dominant as well as African American middle-class culture. The following chapter examines the ways Madam C. J. Walker's early advertisements privileged those same concerns and included issues of economic independence and its primacy in the lives of African American women. In the process, I argue that to understand hair during this period, it is important to look at hairdressing as a business and to attempt to understand what such an option could mean to African American women.

By 1912, Walker claimed to have trained one thousand

women, and when she died in 1919, newspaper articles stated that she had ten thousand women in her employ. Moreover, whereas many other companies appear to have lasted only a few months to a few years, Walker remained in business for a significant period of time and amassed a fortune.

Furthermore, Walker's advertising image could be seen as highly stereotypical. She was a poor, dark-skinned, large-boned African American woman who, until beginning to market hair-care products, had worked as a laundress. Given her circumstances, the possibilities that she would transgress race, class, and gender boundaries in America at the turn of the century were small. Walker used her advertisements to deconstruct this image and attempted to "recode" these visual associations, inserting unconventional associations that repositioned such stereotypical images within the context of her community. Thus, rather than implying that a representation is positive or negative, Walker's ads call for an analysis based on the historical and cultural impetus that gave rise to popular images of African American women as well as a look at "the ways in which black women creators politicize the images."[10]

3

Advertising Contradictions

*M*adam C. J. Walker is credited with widely distributing and popularizing the straightening comb around 1905. This device was one of the first that allowed African American women to change the texture of their hair consistently and make it straight. That the hair did not stay straight was of little concern; what was important was that there was now a method for straightening African American hair that did not have the dangerous side effects of earlier methods. One must then ask, however, whether Walker fulfilled a desire of African American women, or whether she created a desire for her product through marketing and advertising. The answer is that she did both—and so the contradictions begin.

I did not learn about Madam Walker until I was in high school. I had always heard that although she should be celebrated because she was one of the first African American women to make a million dollars, the method by which she made her money was suspect because she preyed on African Americans' feelings of inferiority. As discussed in the previous chapter, African

Americans had long struggled with issues of inferiority, beauty, and the meaning of particular beauty practices carried out in the name of fashion and progress. However, the overlooked portion of this debate involves how Walker, an African American woman, fully aware of the feelings many held toward her chosen profession and desirous of dignifying such practices, resolved these issues for herself; that is, how she shaped her advertisements in a way that allowed other African American women to feel good about using the services she offered and, at the same time, allowed her entrée into the social class of African American women of which she wanted to be a part.

The contradictions involved in Walker's resolution of these issues are the subject of this chapter. Although she popularized the straightening comb, she never mentioned straight hair in any of the advertisements she crafted. Instead, she assumed that African American women would want to straighten their hair and focused on the results of such practices in terms of economic security. In the process, she attempted to shift the significance of hair away from concerns of disavowing African ancestry. Instead, she focused on the realities of many African American women's lives and the way that her new business could offer skills that would make it possible for them to gain a degree of economic independence.

I did not know about Madam Walker when I first decided to straighten my hair. Nor was I thinking about helping my hairdresser (Miss Ruby) gain economic self-sufficiency. However, the issues that Walker presented did embody the contradictions I was attempting to negotiate in my own life during the mid-1970s. I wanted to fit in, to be a part of a particular segment of African American society. I wanted to affirm my African American heritage but be able to experiment with my identity and develop what I believed to be a personal sense of style at the same time. Straightening my hair meant that I would have the opportunity to begin to address these questions, and I wanted to find a way of negotiating concerns about the larger societal ramifications. I desperately needed to believe that I could accomplish all of this and straighten my hair at the same time. This was the real significance of the rhetoric Walker offered in her advertisements: she gave African American women a choice, or a way out, depending on how one looked at it.

Walker advertised heavily in the South and Southwest. She also advertised in selected papers on the East as well as the West Coast, and in 1917 began to target Spanish-language newspapers in Cuba and South America. Receipts indicate that in any given month her advertisements could be found in upward of forty newspapers, and end-of-year records indicate that between 1905 and 1918, she spent anywhere from a few hundred to several thousand dollars on newspaper advertising.[1] Walker's message was widely seen by those who read African American newspapers in various parts of the country.

Her advertisements were widespread enough to enter into dialogue with the dominant society in which she lived as well as with the relatively small group of middle-class African Americans who traditionally controlled the representation of working-class African American women. In her formal advertisements, Walker focused extensively on health and beauty concerns. She spoke exclusively to African American women, whom she assumed looked like her and shared her concerns with beauty and self-sufficiency. However, to accomplish this task, Walker was forced to rearticulate the significance of hegemonic ideologies to allow her message and those ideologies to exist within the same discursive space.

Walker's advertisements relied heavily on a version of her life history designed to highlight her similarities with other working-class African American women. She also foregrounded her success in negotiating class and gender proscriptions within African American culture. That is, to address wide-ranging contradictions, Walker sidestepped many of the criticisms involved in her chosen profession by returning to her accomplishments in overcoming structured inequities associated with gender and class in African American communities. In the end, however, it was all about hair.

Madam C. J. Walker

Madam C. J. Walker was born Sarah Breedlove in Delta, Louisiana, on December 23, 1867. Her parents, Owen and Minerva Breedlove, and two older siblings, Louvenia and Alex, were sharecroppers on a cotton plantation named Grand View. From a young age, Walker worked in the cotton fields alongside her parents and siblings. She was, however, the first member of the family to be born free. In 1874, Owen and Minerva died. The newly orphaned Breedlove children tried to work the land on which they lived, but they were too young to be successful. Sarah's brother, Alex, decided then to move across the river to Vicksburg, Mississippi, to find employment

Finding themselves alone, Sarah and Louvenia took in laundry from white families in town to make a living. Domestic service was one of the few occupations open to African American women, and at that time, doing laundry was almost as backbreaking as sharecropping. Dirty clothes were washed in large wooden tubs, and wooden sticks and washboards were used to beat the soil out of the fabric. Laundresses were paid about one dollar a week by the white families for whom they worked. Thus, by a young age, Walker had experienced two of the primary occupations allowed to working-class African American women—laundress and fieldhand. Therefore, she knew a lot about hard work as well as the rewards that could be expected from such work.

In 1878, yellow fever struck. Between July and November, more than three thousand people around Vicksburg died in the region's worst epidemic. In addition, the cotton crop failed that year. In these extreme circumstances, the Breedlove girls lost their home and joined their brother in Vicksburg, to work as washerwomen. Louvenia was soon married to a man named Willie Powell. Although Sarah was only eleven years old when Lovenia married, she remembered Powell as "cruel and contemptuous." In part to get away from him, Sarah married Moses McWilliams, a laborer in Vicksburg.

On June 6, 1885, when she was seventeen, Sarah gave birth to a daughter, Lelia. Soon after Lelia's second birthday, Moses McWilliams was killed in an accident. At twenty years old, Sarah was a both a widow and a single mother. Although returning to live with her sister may have been offered, the idea of again living with her sister's husband was not an option. Neighbors told her there were jobs for laundresses in St. Louis, Missouri, where wages were higher than those in Vicksburg. She moved in 1887. After arriving, McWilliams joined the St. Paul African Methodist Episcopal Church and became an active member. She was said to have been in awe of the prosperous, well-educated, well-dressed African Americans with whom she came into contact at the church.

These feelings extended to the black leaders McWilliams encountered at the St. Louis World's Fair in 1904. There she saw such African American leaders as Paul Laurence Dunbar, W.E.B. Du Bois, and newspaper publisher T. Thomas Fortune as well as such women as Margaret Murray Washington (the wife of Booker T.) and other members of the National Association of Colored Women. Supposedly struck by the appearance of Margaret Washington, McWilliams began to reflect on her own appearance. She decided that if she improved it, she might gain some of the self-confidence exuded by Washington and other successful African American women.[2]

McWilliams tried a number of patented hair mixtures, including the Poro Company's Wonderful Hair Grower, but with little success. Indeed, for a few months, McWilliams worked as a sales agent for the Poro Company when she was not washing clothes. However, she decided to devise her own hair-care product and go into business for herself. In early 1905, she informed friends that she had learned how to make a product that really worked. Perhaps because she did not want direct competition with the Poro Company, McWilliams decided to leave St. Louis before starting her new business. Her only hesitation about the move seemed to involve her very good friend Charles Joseph Walker, whom she had met and with whom she was falling in love. Nonetheless, she packed her bags and headed for Denver. Her brother had died recently, leaving his widow and four daughters in that city.

McWilliams saved her money carefully and before long had to take in laundry only two days a week. The rest of the time she spent in mixing her products and selling them door to door. A'Lelia Bundles tells us that she "soon proved herself a natural marketer, introducing her products with free demonstrations. After thoroughly washing a woman's hair with her Vegetable Shampoo, she applied her Wonderful Hair Grower, a product that contained medication to combat dandruff and other conditions that sometimes caused hair loss" (40). To complete the treatment, McWilliams applied a light oil to the customer's hair, then pressed it with a heated metal comb. This strategy seemed successful, and her mail order advertisements and personal sales trips were profitable.

In 1910, she and C. J. Walker decided to marry, and together they worked on expanding her business. By the time it was bringing in $10 a week, C. J. Walker decided it had reached its full potential. Sarah Walker, however, decided that if they only knew about it, women all over the country would buy her Wonderful Hair Grower. She and C. J. Walker divorced a few years later over this issue as well as her belief that he wanted to control her company, although she continued to use his name.

Walker used particular aspects of her life history to address societal issues with which many African Americans in general and African American women in particular were confronted. Accordingly, in a letter written to her beauty agents, she suggests that the most successful sales strategy should be a focus on her life: "Acquaint yourself with the history and life of Madam C. J. Walker, get on the very tip of your tongue the strong points that you will find in the story of her personal experience, tell your prospective customer about her, do so in an intelligent and emphatic way, watch his or her face, note what statement or statements impress most, AND THEN DRIVE THE NAIL

HOME" (emphasis hers).[3] Not only are agents encouraged to draw on her personal history, but they are told to do so in a way that is both emphatic and intelligent—they are to see what aspect of Walker's life is most appealing to the customer and use that aspect to actively sell her life story.

The letter goes on to suggest that agents must remember they have something the customer really needs; they should therefore imagine themselves as missionaries trying to convert the unbelievers. Indeed, it was Walker's ability to overcome her proscribed place in American culture that became the grounds upon which she argued that she could be trusted to create a new signification of hair—one that reached beyond the simple relationships between hair and the desire for acceptance from white and middle-class African American culture. For example, in an exchange between Walker and Booker T. Washington, Walker publicly argued for a rearticulation of the significance of hair straightening.

In 1912, Madam C. J. Walker arrived in Chicago to attend the annual convention of the National Negro Business League. Hoping to persuade the league's founder and president, Booker T. Washington, to let her address the gathering of two hundred, she attempted to catch Washington's eye on more than one occasion during the first day's session, but Washington did not acknowledge her. On the second day of the conference, the publisher of the *Indianapolis Freeman,* George Knox, stood and said, "I arise to ask this convention for a few minutes of its time to hear a remarkable woman. She is Madam Walker, the manufacturer of hair goods and preparations." Washington, however, ignored Knox's outburst and continued as if he had not spoken.[4]

Walker decided at that point that she would be heard. The next morning, she again tried to catch Washington's eye, but instead he acknowledged two bankers and looked as though he was about to signal to another businessman when Walker sprang to her feet and said, "Surely you are not going to shut the door in my face. I feel that I am in a business that is a credit to the womanhood of our race. I started in business seven years ago with only $1.50."

As the audience members looked on in surprised silence, probably brought on as much by the unorthodox way in which Walker had begun her testimonial as by the information the speech contained, she continued,

> I am a woman who came from the cotton fields of the South. I was promoted from there to the washtub. Then I was promoted to the cook kitchen, and from there *I promoted myself* into the business of manufacturing hair goods and preparations. I have built my own factory on my own ground. My object in life is not simply to make money for myself or to spend it on myself, I love to use a part of what I make trying to help others. (emphasis hers)

In this short speech, Walker placed herself firmly within the dominant culture's tenet of each person pulling themselves up by their bootstraps and Washington's ideology of racial self-help. This ideology, exemplified by Booker T. Washington, Marcus Garvey, and the socialist W.E.B. Du Bois, held that "every man should strive to become a capitalist . . . the masses should be encouraged to learn trades and professions and that they should be taught that all labor was honorable and a sure road to wealth, that habits of economy and temperance, combined with industry and education would elevate the race."[5]

However, by juxtaposing the role of gender and race constructs in limiting Walker's choices for making money with her initiative in beginning her own company, Walker effectively demonstrates the terrain that must be negotiated if African American women are to participate in the "American dream." As well, her speech highlights the contradictions Walker would have to negotiate for her company to be successful and offers some insight into the task she faced—redefining the meaning of hair in African American communities.

To address these tensions and contradictions, Walker infused her advertisements with a basic philosophy that urged African American women to free themselves from economic dependency on dominant culture and African American men. She counseled women to become hairdressers and make money for themselves, which they should use to help others who were not as fortunate. Walker, therefore, told the audience at the Business League convention that African American women could not remain in their "place" if they wished to advance economically. She also suggested that gender constructs must be redefined.

Unfortunately, many middle-class African American men believed that a woman's place was in the home. Indeed, at the conference, one such African American man argued that "wives should stay at home and take care of their families." Walker responded that "the girls and women of our race must not be afraid to take hold of business endeavor and . . . wring success out of a number of business opportunities that lie at their very doors." Although she made an impression on the delegates, Washington still refused to take any official notice of her or her achievements.

Walker's gender and class appear to have been problematic for Washington. In an angry letter to the editor of a leading African American newspaper, he viewed "with alarm" the tendency of the *New York Age* to advertise hair-straightening products as well as spiritualists and palm readers.[6] He believed that the *Age* reached "too intelligent a *class* of people" (italics mine) to promote such "cheap meaningless stuff."[7] Washington's reference to class was a pointed example of the ways that category functioned to separate positions within the African American community; he himself appeared unconcerned with the prospect of a working or lower class coming into contact with such products. Indeed, his comments presuppose their willingness to use them.

Washington's biographer, Louis T. Harlan, suggests that Washington was opposed to African American cosmetic manufacturers on the grounds that they promoted a white standard of beauty. Washington initially refused to allow any beauty culturists to teach at his vocational training school, Tuskeegee Institute, or to allow owners of firms that produced hair-care products to become members in his National Negro Business League.[8] This position contradicted Washington's ethic of African Americans gaining useful trades and "pulling themselves up by the bootstraps" and was perhaps explained by the fact that most of the owners of these companies were women. As a result, the issues Walker had to unsnarl and address in advertising her new product were daunting. In structuring her advertisements, Walker addressed issues of economic security, class affiliation, migration, and relationships, both personal and professional, with African American men.

The First Advertisement

Walker's first national advertising campaign, begun in 1905, featured a layout that she used for nearly a decade. This particular advertisement was positioned to look like a news article. Indeed, it took up considerably more than half of the page and included a headline and emboldened section headers as well as a two-column format. Because it looked like a news article, it signified the product's reliability and spoke to Walker's trustworthiness. Structuring her advertisement in this way may have reassured readers of the validity of the claims.

At the top of the advertisement are three photographs. The one in the middle is in a rectangular box, and the two on the sides are in ovals. The middle shot shows a young Walker with her hair pulled back over her ears and the front portion of the style curled over her forehead. Her hair looks about three to four inches long and the words "Before Using" are superimposed over the bottom of the box. The two side photographs picture an older Walker. One shows Walker's profile, while the other pictures her looking directly into the camera. In the two latter photographs, her hair falls well below her shoulders. Although the word "after" is not written on or below these photographs, it is clear from the length of the hair that some time has passed. In the "before" photograph, Walker does not look directly into the camera but looks down and off to the side.

Although this photograph was probably not taken specifi-cally for advertising purposes, her choices are worthy of com-ment. The "before" photograph suggests that short hair inter-fered with Walker's sense of self-worth to the extent that she could not look the world (or here, the camera) in the eye. How-ever, once Walker's hair has grown, she looks boldly into the camera. Hair growth has altered her sense of self. In this way, "before" and "after" take on ideological significance as Walker illustrates for readers that hair growth is key to feelings of de-fiance and resistance.

As a result, whereas Walker refrains from offering critiques of racial features, the placement of these photographs suggests subtly that a change in hair length will change the ways African American women function in the world. The change, however, will not be characterized by acceptance within the dominant culture but rather will consist of enhanced internal feelings of self-pride and resistance to that culture. Because the image on the left looks forward, Walker is able to see both her past, as represented by the older image of herself, and her future. The image on the right looks out at the world. She has become the person she wants to be.

Although we may read Walker's choice and placement of photographs in this way, the remainder of the advertising text does not make such explicit connections. Instead, the headline reads, "It Makes Short Hair Long and Cures Dandruff." The "cure" here is not predicated on the user's desire to funda-mentally change her physical characteristics but rather on a wish to be free of scalp conditions and dandruff. The product does not cure social inequality but will help with conditions that Walker contends are an impediment to hair growth. As a result, Walker begins to fashion an ideology that masks beauty regimes as a health cure. The advertisement goes on to say that for eighteen years, she unsuccessfully tried different products said to beautify African American hair, when, "through the Divine Providence of God I was permitted in a dream to discover the preparation that I am now placing at the disposal of the thousands who are today in the same condition that I was in, just three years ago. . . . Consequently, I left Denver to place my goods on the market, and in reach of those who appreciate beautiful hair and healthy scalps, which is the glory of woman" (*Indianapolis Ledger,* 1906).

Walker speaks to African American women as a fellow sufferer from the problems her product will cure. Because her hair grower worked for her, it will work for them; "after all," she seems to say, "I am no different from you." At the same time, her reasons for advertising her "discovery" evoke a type of evangelical zeal. She tells readers that God not only answered her prayers to find a product that would work but singled her out by actually speaking to her in a dream. Because of "Divine Providence," she is now spreading the word to others. To ensure that the connection between God and her product is not missed, Walker invokes the biblical text that refers to hair as a woman's crown and glory.

Walker's "creation story" speaks to African American women in a number of ways. To support her efforts was to affirm a religious experience. In much the same way as the biblical figure Deborah begins to preach and teach Scripture after having been visited in a dream by God, Walker likens her constant traveling and speeches about African American women's beauty to this same type of quest. In organizing her argument around religious and biblical signs, Walker places her relationship with church doctrine within an easily recognizable context. Her story about the way the company was begun, whether true or not, is a part of the discourse Walker constructed to attract buyers for her products. At different times in her business life, and in different places in the African American community, she called on one or more of these basic elements of her beginnings, or the company's creation story. She chose consistently to highlight the divine intervention that made the formula for the product possible. She then juxtaposed the "heavenly" with the "earthly" by discussing why selling the product could make women's lives more productive on earth—by freeing them from work as a laundresses or domestics.

The advertisement ends with nine letters from "satisfied customers," which, we are told, were unsolicited. The letter writers begin by stating that once their hair was in terrible condition but now it is growing nicely, and all thanks to Walker and her product. All of the letters are from African American women, and many ask to be allowed to sell Walker's products in their hometowns. Again, the rhetoric of inclusion and similarity between the product's creator, its various users, and its potential customers is underscored. Straightening hair however, is, not mentioned.

Given the views of African American intellectuals and leaders regarding the problems with advocating hair straightening as a way of finding acceptance within American society, it is significant that Walker answers these charges by creating a loud silence in her advertisements. She also consistently asked editors and writers to refrain from using the term "hair straightener" when writing about her in their newspapers and magazines. In one interview Walker made her position on hair straightening perfectly clear. When the reporter asked her about her rise to fame as a hair straightener, Walker responded, "Right here let me correct the erroneous impression held by some that I claim to straighten the hair. I want the great masses of my people to take a greater pride in their personal appearance and to give their hair proper attention. . . . I dare say that in the next ten years it will be a rare thing to see a kinky head of hair and it will not be straight either."[9]

Whereas Walker's assertion that African American women would cease to straighten their hair within the next ten years did not prove prophetic, this statement speaks to one of the undergirding tenets of her treatment. Walker considered the ritual of her system as important as the actual hairstyle. She instructed her agents to create an atmosphere in which African American women would feel pampered and valued while giv-

ing the hair "proper attention." Indeed, agents interested in the
Walker system of treatment learned a philosophy of inner as
well as outer beauty.

Beauty, they were taught, referred to outer manifestations
such as physical cleanliness and good health as well as to inner
things such as mental cleanliness. In addition, her beauty handbook suggests that operators were to be soothing and relaxing
during conversation and that they should always "secure absolute rest for the patron if she is to get the most beneficial results."[10] Walker considered the ritual of her system to be as
important as the actual hairstyle, thus shifting the terrain of the
debate over hair straightening from dissatisfaction with African
physical features to a focus on health as well as physical and
mental well-being. Walker did not argue that there was nothing
wrong with African American women straightening their hair;
she flat out denied that hair straightening was what she had to
offer.

In a letter to her business partner and attorney, F. B. Ransom,
Walker writes that she is enclosing a clipping from the *Post
Dispatch* in which they referred to her as both a "negress" and a
hair straightener. She is upset because she thought the writer
would have known better than to refer to her as a negress, but she
specifically asked him not to refer to her as a hair straightener.
Also, in 1914, she began to run an advertisement that said, "Do
not handle false hair nor straightening tongs. No curling irons;
an entirely new method used. No burning or singeing, but a
beautiful head of hair in *natural* condition" (*New York Age,* 1914).

Walker appealed to potential customers to disregard concerns about hair straightening and the political nature of such
an act and see for themselves what she had to offer. She was also
eager to point out that she was willing and able to treat hair that
had not been straightened. If potential customers were inclined
to believe that she saw herself as duplicating services offered by
other hair culturists, who often advertised their services as
being able to straighten African American hair, she took great
pains to disabuse them of this idea.

Her desire to distance herself from assertions that she was only concerned with changing the natural texture of the hair speaks to a level of ambivalence or perhaps to a degree of political consciousness on Walker's part. On the one hand, she wished to appeal to African American women to purchase her product. On the other, she wanted to distance herself from attacks on hair straightening as a self-destructive practice. It appears that she addressed this tension by changing her strategy to emphasize exclusively the possibility that other African American women would make money for themselves by learning her particular method of hair preparation as well as becoming distributors of her products.

For example, in an ad that began to appear in late 1914, Walker touts her system of hair care as "a real opportunity for women who wish to become independent." She adds that her hair preparations are giving support to "more than 1,000,000 people in this industry." Walker's juxtaposition of "real" with "imagined" independence speaks to concerns with economic self-sufficiency and positions her as having contributed to the racial "uplift" of the African American masses. Later that same year, Walker began to command women to "Learn to Grow Hair and Make Money" because "A Diploma from Lelia College of Hair Culture Is Your Passport to Prosperity" (fig. 6).

In this ad, the earlier triad of photographs has been replaced with a large "glamour shot" of Walker. She is wearing earrings, a necklace, and a fringed shawl. Her image has been softened by the way her body is positioned in relationship to the camera. No longer does she stare defiantly out at the world but looks down demurely. The bold message of economic self-sufficiency and prosperity for African American women is mediated by the visual image of what a woman who attempts to move from her societally proscribed place into the business world looks like. She is pretty, feminine, demure, well dressed, and has straight hair.

Walker's decision to market economic self-sufficiency through use of a nonthreatening advertising image is signifi-

Learn To Grow Hair and Make Money

Complete Course by mail or by personal instructions. A diploma from Leila College of Hair Culture is a passport to prosperity. Is your hair short, breaking off, thin or falling out? Have you tetter, eczema? Does your scalp itch? Have you more than a normal amount of dandruff?

MME. C. J. WALKER'S

Wonderful Hair Grower

Write for booklet which tells of the positive cures of all scalp diseases, stops the hair from falling out and starts it at once to growing.

Beware of imitations—all of the Mme. C. J. Walker Preparations are put up in yellow tin boxes.

A six weeks' trial treatment sent to any address by mail for $1.50. Make all money orders payable to Mme. C. J. Walker. Send stamps for reply. **Agents Wanted. Write for terms.**

MADAM C. J. WALKER
President of the Madam C. J. Walker Manufacturing Company and the Leila College,. 640 N. West Street, Indianapolis, Ind.

See your nearest Walker Agent or Write

THE MADAM C. J. WALKER MFG. CO.

640 North West Street,   Indianapolis, Ind.

Fig. 6. Learn to grow hair.

cant. This period in African American history was marked by resounding calls for a broadening of African American women's participation in the public sphere, as defined by political involvement, and a critique of ideologies that placed African American women solely within the home. For example, in her 1892 book-length feminist analysis of the condition of blacks, especially women, Anna J. Cooper wrote, "Fifty years ago woman's activity according to orthodox definitions was in a pretty clearly cut 'sphere,' including primarily the kitchen and the nursery. . . . The woman of today finds herself in the presence of responsibilities which ramify through the profoundest and most varied interests of her country and race."[11] She was joined in her assessment by Fannie Barrier Williams, who argued that "We are living, in what may be called a woman's age. The old notion that woman was intended by the Almighty to do only those things that men thought they ought to do, is fast passing away. In our day . . . a woman's sphere is just as large as she can make it. . . . Her world is constantly becoming larger . . . by virtue of her wider influence and larger participation in human affairs" (97).

Although there were some who advocated a widening of spheres for African American women, there were others who believed that although women were capable of participating in public life, their first responsibility was to home and family. Josephine Washington points out that some African American women "have never sought to extend their influence beyond the domestic circle and others who have are being scorned." She goes on to caution that a woman who chooses to enter the public sphere must not neglect her domestic duties. In describing the qualities one needs to balance these two ideals, she writes that such a woman is

> modest and womanly, with a reverence for the high and holy duties of wife and mother. She does not advocate the abandonment of any real duties at hand for fancied ones afar off. She would not have women neglect home and husband and children to enter professional life, or to further any public cause, however worthy. [However] contact with the outer world, a little rubbing against other minds . . . refreshes and invigorates the tired wife and mother and enables her to give her best to the dear ones at home.[12]

Washington positions participation in the public sphere in relation to the private and argues that a woman should participate in the world outside of the home because this will give her the energy she needs to be a better wife and mother. Whereas Washington advocates a stance that allows for African American women's participation in public life as long as that participation did not interfere with "any real duties," many African American men decried any public involvement whatsoever for African American women.

In an editorial entitled "How to Keep Women at Home," Fred Moore writes that it is apparent that women's excursions from home are causing men great discomfort. He argues, "The tendency of the modern woman to 'gad about' is a problem that mere man finds difficult of solution. . . . They are on the street, in the club . . . in the theaters, in societies, in the lecture rooms . . . everywhere but home."[13] He suggests that men call a convention so that they can devise a solution to this problem. Moore's distress at African American women's desire to leave the domestic sphere is echoed by Thomas Nelson Baker:

> The hope of the race is conditioned not upon the woman on the platform, but upon the woman in the home—not upon the women whose highest ambition is to appear in public and pass resolutions about the race, but upon the mothers whose highest ambition is not to show themselves and make public speeches, but whose highest ambition is to give the best there is in them to their children . . . the hope of the race is conditioned upon that class of women who are too busy with their children to attend conventions. . . . One thing the education of the Negro woman must not do, it must not educate her away from being a mother—it must not be an education that will maker her feel there is a higher sphere for women than that of being a mother.[14]

Baker's obvious anxiety at the numbers of African American women who appear to be choosing a life for themselves at the imagined expense of their husbands and children is a clear indication that the practice caused tensions within African American communities. While some argued that the time had long passed when women could be expected to stay within the domestic sphere, others suggested a combination of the two; yet still others decried the presence of African American women in any sphere but the domestic.

As a result, Walker had many obstacles to overcome in the process of legitimizing her newly formed business as well as attracting African American women to this same pursuit—she had to negotiate gender and class proscriptions in African American communities as well as appease members of the African American community who disagreed with the types of service she offered and did not want African American women to engage in business practices outside of the home. To do all this, Walker relied on visual images of her body, which reinscribed ideologies of gender and femininity; at the same time, she advocated women moving out of the domestic sphere to make money for themselves.

Walker connected learning to grow hair with prosperity by encouraging women to become Walker agents and open up a beauty parlor. Often these "parlors" were located in private homes, but many women rented out space in established beauty parlors or opened their own parlors. After graduating from Lelia College, or from the mail-order course, women were allowed to use the Walker name in any advertisements. However, they could only use Walker products in their shops and could not practice any other system of hair treatment, such as Madame Poro's. Walker thus sought to dominate the marketplace by selling products as well as by training others to sell her products.

Ideological Shifts: Later Advertisements

Beginning in late 1917, Walker's advertisements shifted again to deemphasize image and instead to focus on the international scope of her product as well as on the overall size of the company. This theme is taken up in one of the last advertisements Walker was responsible for placing before her death. In it is a map of North as well as South America, with tins of Walker's products placed over both continents. The headline reads, "A Million Eyes Turned Upon it Daily." This advertisement includes a sketch of Walker in the lower left-hand corner and a group of men and women in the lower right-hand corner with their eyes upturned toward the Walker Company logo, which

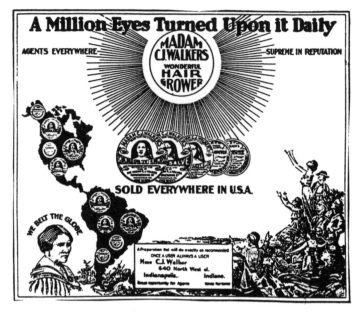

Fig. 7. A million eyes.

occupies the center of the advertisement. The product is said to be "Supreme in Reputation" (fig. 7).

Walker infuses this advertisement with religious overtones, as the group of people in the corner raise their arms heavenward, toward the company logo, which is in the middle of the page. Walker also seems to suggest a type of cultural "uplift" for those in North and South America who have the privilege of gazing on her products. As a result, this advertisement speaks to "culture building" through product distribution.

At this time, Walker began to structure advertisements that deemphasized economics and images of African American women, perhaps because she was becoming more aware of politics in her own life. These shifts in ideological undergirding are significant in that they speak to the ways ideology constructs advertising and its effect on issues of representation within an African American cultural discourse.

Between 1916 and 1919, Walker engaged in a number of activities that characterized this awareness. In April 1916, she wrote letters indicating that she wished to organize her cosmetics agents into a union. In 1917, Walker wrote that she intended to socialize her company (although there is no evidence to suggest that she was ever a socialist) and was preparing to embark upon a trip to a peace conference as a delegate for the International League of Darker Peoples. She also began to campaign on behalf of various socialist candidates.[15]

Walker's interest in union organizing grew out of a desire to protect her agents from tariffs and price controls. She wanted to organize African American cosmetic manufacturers for the same purpose, and in 1917 she organized the National Negro Cosmetic Manufacturers Association. The cosmetic manufacturers' union was intended to aid association members with buying product ingredients and advertising in newspapers and periodicals. It also set standards for price and quality of the product that served to protect the manufacturer as well as the purchaser from poor-quality goods. Here Walker applied scientific management practices common in the Progressive Era and its politics. The minutes of the meeting add that quality and price protection were "every ones first aim instead of the money to be gained wherein it has been so often the case that the white man who is not interested in Colored Women's Beauty only looks to further his own gains and puts on the market preparations that are absolutely of no aid whatsoever to the Skin, Scalp or Hair."[16] Given that these companies were not particularly large, the association members were more concerned with their incomes and protecting their markets from intrusion by white competitors than they were with their workers. The manufacturers thought this was necessary because they believed "the white man" neither knew about nor cared for "Colored Women's Beauty."

This rationale implied that African American women and men who manufactured beauty products were in a better position to care for African American hair, skin, and scalp. These manufacturers articulated a stance that presupposed that their race implied an inherent ability to produce products that would best beautify African American women. Again, the rhetoric of similarity and inclusion operated as a rationale for purchasing one product over another. Walker also offered an analysis of the ways class was an important factor in choosing products. Here she aligned herself with those who argued that middle- and upper-class African Americans wished to keep the working class from benefiting from such products.

Toward that end, in July 1918, Walker's acquaintance and sometime employee Louis George wrote an article in *The Messenger* entitled "Beauty Culture and Colored People." In it George argues that those who advocate the use of beauty products designed specifically for African American women do so because of the economic benefits as well as the "vague aesthetic idea" that what makes one look better ought to be used. He concludes that the "practice of beauty culture" is a proper concern for African American women. George was not only a friend of Walker's but the secretary of the newly formed Negro Cosmetic Manufacturers Association.[17]

In the article, George criticizes editors and lecturers who decry the use of such products based on the argument that people should be "natural" when they themselves go to great lengths to effect the look that they find most pleasing. He believes these critics would deny this opportunity to the "masses" of African American women. Speaking to issues of class and the relationship of the African American middle class to "the masses," he suggests that middle-class editors and lecturers are capable of dictating the behavior of those who do not share their economic or class background. Like Walker, George grounds his defense of cosmetic manufacturers in economic concerns, which he believes justify the manufacture and marketing of beauty products.

If African American women can gain some level of economic independence by marketing these products, then, as far as George is concerned, they should continue. Indeed, he quotes figures on the amount of money that women of European descent spent on cosmetics and beauty-related products and implies that it is only reasonable that someone should attempt to benefit from supplying these same types of products to African American women. As a result of this rhetoric, Walker's later advertisements make much more explicit her desire to cultivate working-class African American women as a new group of customers.

In one of the last advertisements she created, Walker proclaims that her products are used everywhere; her photograph is superimposed over a map of the United States, and the distribution sites as well as the supply centers are indicated. The copy claims that Walker's products are "Sold Everywhere in the U.S.A." This advertisement is one of the few that pictures or discusses any product other than her hair grower. In it there are tins of her Tetter Salve, Vegetable Shampoo, and Glossine. However, the Glossine is positioned last in a row of tins, and it is difficult to read the label. Whereas the product is mentioned, it is certainly not emphasized.

The insert in the advertisement says, "You will Eventually Use the Treatments and Preparations So Why Not Now." Here Walker has switched to focus on the size of her company and appears to have decided to eschew any discussion of health, beauty, and/or the monetary benefits of an alliance with her. She also appears to be attempting to indicate a national audience by including a map with lines emanating from her headquarters in Indianapolis. Because Walker used a photograph of herself in every advertisement up to this point, there can be no doubt by anyone reading these advertisements that the company is headed by an African American woman. As a result, she broadened the boundaries of representations of African American women and pictured them as concerned with a wider range of issues than was usually considered.

Printed advertisements were only one part of Walker's overall marketing strategy. She traveled extensively to promote her products, speaking in churches, schools, and lodges and coming into contact with a wide range of African American women. During these trips, she mounted major advertising campaigns in the local African American newspapers in the cities she visited. As a result, women were influenced as much by Walker's presence and her speeches as by the advertisement itself.

Walker fashioned a number of discourses and strategies to help her negotiate the terrains of gender and class in dominant as well as African American communities. Looking at these various strategies allows, indeed forces, us to refrain from viewing race, class, gender, and their ideologies as discrete constructs that can be analyzed separately in the lives of African American women. The meaning of hair came to be inseparable from such concerns. This is evident in Walker's advertisements, which highlight similarities as well as differences between Walker and the women she identified as her target audience.

4

Broadening Representational Boundaries

Throughout most of the nineteenth century, middle-class African American intellectuals championed hair in its natural state as the preferred style for group members. By the mid-1920s, however, straight hair had become the preferred texture to signal middle-class status. This preference remained constant for decades to come. Indeed, as late as 1976, my grandmother believed I would be ostracized by middle-class African Americans if I did not straighten my hair.

I cannot be absolutely sure why she believed straight hair signaled respect and acceptance from a certain class of African Americans. Neither can I pinpoint definitively when the shift took place. I do know, however, that following World War I, hairdressers came to be considered solidly middle class, and hairdressing became a respectable career. I also know that Madam C. J. Walker carefully crafted and distributed an image designed to undermine class-based arguments against both straight hair and hairdressing.

This chapter examines the image Walker shaped and controlled and argues that by manufacturing a place for herself in African American communities that was usually occupied by celebrities or stars, she helped to problematize class-based assumptions about the meaning of hair. She was able to reconfigure what constituted an "acceptable" representation of an African American woman within the public sphere, and her identity construction challenged hegemonic ideologies of education and domesticity as the sole indicators of class status. Whereas representations of Walker's body and image in hair advertisements are certainly cultural texts and, as such, indicate a means of coming to understand her significance, her widespread promotion of that visual image through different media is equally significant.

Specifically, although Walker was interested in aligning herself with middle-class African American business and intellectual leaders as a method to boost her product visibility, she remained suspicious of the motivations behind efforts to "uplift the masses" and to position middle-class identity as the sole model of success and leadership. Walker's celebrity image allowed her to create a place for herself from which she was able to propose alternative definitions of success, while at the same time distributing her message about the meaning and possible rewards of hair in African American communities.

During and and after World War I, African American communities were buffeted by competing ideologies of identity. Such writers and orators as J. A. Rogers and Marcus Garvey stood on street corners expounding upon the beauty and strength found in an African heritage. In addition to Garvey's exhortations of "Back to Africa" and "Africa for Africans," W.E.B. Du Bois, in the pages of the liberal bourgeois National Association for the Advancement of Colored People's *Crisis* magazine, voiced "Pan-Africanist" concerns.

Membership and support for Garvey's black nationalist Universal Negro Improvement Association (UNIA) grew quickly between World War I and the early 1920s. The paid membership in the UNIA is difficult to ascertain, but it was Garvey's influence, his voicing of the generally ignored hopes of the masses of African Americans, that give his movement its place in history. Garvey believed that African American people in the United States would never be treated fairly and should return to their African homeland. Short of this, he encouraged and established several African American–owned and –run businesses. He thought it important for African American girls to play with African American dolls, and one of his manufacturing concerns produced them. Historians who are sympathetic as well as those ideologically opposed to Garvey's program concur that his was the largest mass movement in African American history—testament to the fact that his message of African American self-determination was heard by the "folk," not just the middle classes.

In his newspaper, the *Negro World*, Garvey refused advertisements from companies that promoted the straightening of African American hair as well as the lightening of African American skin. Like his mentor, Booker T. Washington, he railed against African American newspapers that accepted such advertisements, arguing that such products attempted "to make a new race and make a monkey out of the Negro."[1] Interestingly, he found it necessary to appeal to Madam C. J. Walker for support of his early organizational efforts.

African American Female Identity: The War Years

After World War I, within mainstream popular culture African Americans were closely identified with exoticism. The white avant-garde of the Roaring Twenties believed African Americans were the embodiment of exotic primitivism and that they did not have the sexual restraints and repressions that so worried Freud and others ready to exit the sexual confines of the Victorian era. To help them release their own sexual inhibitions, upper- and middle-class whites started "slumming." In New York City, for example, they could "take the A train" uptown to visit Harlem and such entertainment spots as the Cotton Club.

There they could gaze on chorus lines made up of "high yellow," scantily clad African American women whose hair was straight and who, for patrons of these clubs, exemplified sexual freedom and exoticism.

Within African American communities, however, there was a very different discussion taking place regarding what African American women symbolized and the proper image they should project to the world. Most often, that image centered around a certain class of African American. For example, in the September 2, 1917, *New York Times Magazine,* an article titled "The Wealthiest Negro Colony in the World" foregrounded the economic progress made by notable African Americans, including Madam C. J. Walker. In chronicling their lifestyles, the article notes the presence of "liveried servants, sometimes foreign-born whites . . . in the more pretentious homes."

In the article, we are told that no less than 250 "Negroes" own their own homes, that many own automobiles, some even have chauffeurs, and that many count their fortunes in the six figures. In Harlem, African Americans who choose to work hard are rewarded with prosperity. In Harlem, there is a class of "Negro" that, because of the members' business success, may be described as "both alert and progressive." In Harlem, the article tells us, African Americans may be best understood by looking at a professional class that provides services and merchandise to ensure the "convenience, comfort and pleasure" of all.

In support of this statement, the article informs readers that the churches run butcher shops and grocery stores and that at least one congregation is committed to purchasing a house every month, which they will remodel and rent to recent immigrants from the South. A stock company and a chain of twelve drugstores are owned by African Americans as well as movie theaters and vaudeville houses. The article also names beauty parlors as a type of business that thrives in "the zone" and notes that "the stranger gets the idea that many members of the colored race must be afflicted with baldness, or think that their hair needs some sort of treatment."

The author explains that one woman amassed a fortune from

her hair preparations, adding, "She and her daughter own and occupy a large house in West 136th Street. It was built recently and with its furnishings, probably cost about $50,000. The owner is called the wealthiest Negro woman in the country. Fourteen years ago she was a washerwoman." Although unnamed, the woman is Madam Walker.

What is crucial here is the way the article connects the idea of progress for all African Americans with the business success and consumption patterns of a few. As a result, Walker comes to represent the possibility of moving from the lower rungs to society's apex, and her successful transcendence of lower- or working-class boundaries is exemplified by her wealth. This image of Walker is replicated in an article published the following month in the *Literary Digest*, titled "Queen of Gotham's Colored 400."[2]

The article begins by stating that "Fourteen years ago Mrs. Walker was earning her living at the washtub. Today she is the richest negress in New York." Because the article begins by juxtaposing Walker's past class position with her present circumstances, we are led to believe that it is this movement that is most significant. We are then told how much she spent for her present home and that she is in the process of building a new house that will cost a quarter of a million dollars. The article ends with a discussion of how much Walker spends to furnish her surroundings. We find out that her bedroom furnishings cost $4,500 and that she has two gold-leaf Victrolas that cost $200 a piece.

Although neither article relates Walker to the class of elite African Americans who identified themselves as "New Negros," the sketch of life and business in Harlem and the profile of Walker foreground key tenets of this trope, which functioned in important ways to measure racial "progress" for the group by the class position of a few. Within African American communities, this trope was constructed to function as a model that others should emulate in attempting to better their condition within the larger American society.[3]

These portrayals of Walker appear to fit neatly into a paradigm that emphasized class difference as grounds for recognition and acceptance from the dominant culture, and her success was certainly a model others might hope to follow. Indeed, she is singled out as an "exemplary" member of an "exemplary" class. However, the dominant press's promotion of Walker's wealth and background was strikingly different from the ways in which "New Negro" ideologists constructed a public image for themselves, particularly their women.

For example, in 1900, Booker T. Washington helped edit a volume titled *A New Negro for a New Century.* The volume included a picture and biography of Mrs. Booker T. Washington, principal of the women's program at Tuskeegee Institute, and noted her work with African American women's clubs. There is also a picture and article about Mrs. Ida Gray Nelson, "the only Colored lady dentist in the country who is graduate of the University of Michigan at Ann Arbor." Also included are a "prominent teacher of physical culture in the schools of Washington D.C." and Fannie Barrier Williams, a newspaper columnist, author, and member of the Chicago Woman's Club.

The women singled out in this volume exhibit similar qualities. They are all "professional" women who have achieved a certain social standing due to their education and middle-class backgrounds. They exemplify the view held by Claudia White that African American women can "prove to the world that Negro womanhood when properly treated and educated will burst forth into gems of pure brilliancy unsurpassed by any other gems among any other race."[4] As a result of such opinions, representations of African American women in the public sphere tended to portray middle-class women who illustrated what allegiance to hegemonic ideals surrounding education and class status could do.

Four years later, in an essay titled "A Study of the Features of the New Negro Woman," the author saw fit to reproduce visual images of seven ideal "New Negro" women, with captions that explained why the women had been chosen. One caption reads that Gussie is "An admirer of Fine Art, a performer on the violin and the piano, a sweet singer, a writer—mostly given to essays, a lover of good books, and a home making girl." Another tells us that Lorainetta is a "model girl, the result of careful home training and steady schooling." Whereas the first volume saw fit to praise its "New Negro" women for their business achievements and work outside the home, the other focused on women most concerned with domesticity and liberal education. In both cases, however, education was key.[5]

Walker, a sharecropper's daughter with a third grade education, divorced from two husbands, and given to constant travel, did not fit neatly into an ideology that emphasized education and domesticity as a prerequisite for "New Negro" status. And hairdressing was certainly not the career that other members of this group chose for themselves. In addition, her arguments that African American women, no matter what their class background, should enter the public sphere as businesswomen threatened to alienate her from influential members of that group. As a result, she was forced to highlight alternative characteristics in articulating her significance and relationship to African American communities. These characteristics centered predominantly on her wealth. Indeed, when one looks closely at her practice of identity construction, it becomes clear that the previously mentioned articles merely drew on an aspect of her image that she carefully crafted and distributed widely. However, whereas these articles used Walker to illustrate the possibility of racial progress for all African Americans, Walker's self-authored articles in the African American press posit a different meaning of her image. These functioned to position her as a celebrity existing outside of traditional definitions of class.

Celebrity Image and the African American Press

Like others, Walker frequently wrote articles about herself, which she submitted to African American newspapers for publication. Although a few editors balked at the practice as "creat-

Fig. 8. Self-authored article.

ing news" and offered to run the press releases as an advertisement if she would pay the advertising fee, most editors and publishers, mindful of the huge amounts of money she spent in actual advertising, ran the story as asked.[6] These types of articles often appeared on pages that carried her advertisements and those for other hair products. Because readers had no way of knowing that the article had been authored by Walker, her image was enhanced as an African American woman important enough to have her activities chronicled by the press (fig. 8).

In these articles, Walker focused extensively on her charitable gifts, recent purchases, and travel. Almost every time that she purchased a piece of property or a new car, donated more than $100 to a charitable organization, or traveled out of state, the activity appeared as a self-authored article in various African American newspapers. One such article, appearing in the *New York Age,* alerted readers that Walker had just returned from a tour of New England, where she spoke before large audiences.[7] It also revealed that many social courtesies were extended to her everywhere she went and ended by telling readers that in the next few months she planned to move her residence from Indianapolis to New York.

Such articles are strikingly similar to those that appeared on the society page, which discussed the travels of upper-class African Americans familiar to the communities in which the newspaper was published. However, in maneuvering to have this article printed on a page with "hard" news, Walker raised the level of her activities beyond mere neighborhood status and shaped an identity that was at once hers alone and at the same time worthy of note because of her membership in a racial group. Indeed, the underlying purpose was to connect wealth with Walker's importance to the larger community.

The article mentioned above went on to chronicle the amount of money Walker planned to spend on the New York property and its furnishings. Readers are told that she put down $10,000 cash on a $40,000 piece of property and would use between $10,000 and $20,000 to remodel. She had already purchased a dining parlor suite for $2,850 and a bedroom suite valued at $2,220. Lastly, the article states that a prominent young New York society matron would be engaged as her social secretary and would be paid a liberal salary.

Walker constructed herself as a part of "society" constituted by education, breeding, standing, and wealth, and as such, she was someone able to offer employment to "prominent society matrons." As a result, she positioned the doctrine of racial uplift in relationship to an elite group of middle- and upper-class

African Americans whom she employed, as opposed to just the lower and working classes. At the same time, Walker's transcendence of class boundaries is underscored.

In another article, she wrote yet again about purchasing an estate, this one located at Irvington-on-Hudson. Walker's choice of location is important because Irvington, located just outside New York City, is described in the article as "One of the richest areas in the country," and readers are informed that Walker has chosen to locate her residence there because "wealthy white residents" in a less fashionable area refused to let her buy an estate in their neighborhood. Because of this initial refusal, Walker decided to purchase an estate in the most prestigious area she could find, and she chose not to publicize her new purchase until renovations on the property were nearing completion.

The article begins by congratulating her on her new purchase and moves on to state that everyone knows that "Madame Walker has always been original, independent, fearless in her investments, and from time to time has surprised and electrified the reading public, by some great gift or big investment. But the fact being generally conceded that Madame Walker's business is the greatest of its kind in the country and that her financial resources are almost unlimited, we have just about reached the state, where no venture on her part would startle or surprise."[8] Although the article is supposed to be about Walker's purchase of a piece of property, it also begins to construct an identity for her that highlights specific characteristics. She describes herself as "original, independent, fearless" and capable of "surprising and electrifying the reading public." The article functions as a clearly worded rationale for Walker's insistence on highlighting her material possessions and business achievements. Indeed, in explaining her reasons for focusing so completely on her earnings and possessions, Walker asserted, "it is my accumulations that have brought me into the limelight and this side interests [audiences] most."[9]

These articles never mention Walker's previous class background or the route that brought her to this point. As a result, she emerges fully formed to articulate her beliefs about the significance of her wealth for African Americans. In one instance, she went so far as to proclaim, "Every age has its great men or women and this is true of every people. No unbiased historian can chronicle the history of the Negro without weaving the name of Madam C. J. Walker into the warp and woof of its life and institutions here in America."[10] Walker saw herself as a star. As such, she invited newspaper readers to direct their attention from earthly concerns to wonder at her sparkle and brilliance. Because she wanted to inspire individuals with the story of how she had overcome economic hardships to become prosperous and upwardly mobile, Walker focused on the amounts of money she was able to earn and spend, and she positioned this consumption as a rationale for dignifying the practice of hairdressing.

Although stars are usually understood as movie actors and actresses whose image formation includes their films as well as the information publicly available about them, one might extend the term to include all celebrities who are objects of media construction. Richard Dyer defines a star's image as the result of promotion of the star's films and the star's persona through pinups, public appearances, studio handouts, and so on, as well as interviews, biographies, and coverage in the press of the star's doings and "private" life. Further, a star's image includes what others say or write about him or her, the way the image is used in such contexts as advertisements, novels, and pop songs, and finally, the way the star can become part of everyday speech. Star images, for Dyer, are always extensive, multimedia, and intertextual. They are created for the sake of profit and may be used to sell products. As a result, the image is as much of a commodity as the products it helps to sell.[11] Walker's practices of image construction, self-image distribution, and her use of that image function as a star image.

Walker used her position as a star in African American communities to attract business to her company as well as to aid community groups with various projects. In a letter dated February 22, 1918, Walker writes that the clubwomen in Pittsburgh have asked her to appear as an attraction at a "big affair" for the old folks' home they are planning.[12] By agreeing to appear at public functions as an "attraction," she attempted to help such groups raise money. Although in the beginning she herself did not always make money for her appearances, she believed they would help the business in the long run.[13] Perhaps she was right, because in 1918 she began to charge a twenty-five-cent admission fee for public lectures, and on at least one occasion, she made $150 after expenses.[14] Walker's self-authored articles probably helped to ensure attendance at these lectures, and at the same time, these lectures guaranteed an interest in her products. In this way, these discursive constructions of her image functioned together to create an overall signification.

Whereas her newspaper articles and public lectures afforded Walker widespread distribution of her image, she devised other methods as well to heighten her visibility. For most of her career, Walker traveled at least thirty-eight weeks out of the year. In October 1915, however, due to the strain constant traveling placed on her health and because she wanted to cover more of the country, Walker hired three special agents to help her perform these tasks. These special agents distributed the image, message, and product of Madam Walker and were paid $100 a month. Agents were to "travel . . . from place to place, teaching the art of hair culture and . . . to advertise and represent the business and goods of Madam C. J. Walker."[15] Not only did they teach Walker's method of hair treatment, they also represented her image and were responsible for distributing that image as they traveled.

At times she directed agents to concentrate on specific areas, but most often she left them to their own devices and allowed them to choose the areas of the country and the towns they wished to visit. No records exist that pinpoint how many lectures Walker and these women gave in a given period of time, but in one month, Walker traveled from Mexico to Los Angeles to San Francisco to Oakland, to Seattle and Tacoma, and then back to Los Angeles. On the average, she gave one speech a night. During this same period she had at least five special agents who kept this same pace.[16]

Walker and her agents also made a point of attending religious conventions to advertise her image and sell her products. For example, in 1915 she was concerned that renovations on a piece of property she owned in Flushing, New York, be rushed to make sure that members of the African Methodist Episcopal conference would be able to meet her there. She also wanted the property ready so that the Women's Federation attendees could come up from Baltimore: "I was planning to have them run one day's excursions down to Flushing; and I feel that would be a big ad for me."[17] This practice of soliciting clients from religious conventions continued. In August 1917, Alice Burnett writes that she is leaving for the Baptist Convention as instructed. A few days later she writes to ask for more supplies because business is going quite well.[18]

The A.M.E. and Black Baptists constituted the majority of African Americans with religious affiliations, and in 1916, the Black Baptist Convention was ranked the third largest religious body in the United States after the Roman Catholic and Methodist Episcopal churches. According to Evelyn Brooks-Higginbotham, this denomination formed a "microcosm of the black population in America and included men and women from all social classes and geographic regions."[19] As a result of appearing personally at such functions or sending an agent in her place, Walker had access to many African American women from varying class backgrounds. This went far toward dignifying hairdressing as a career for the women who participated in such conferences, not to mention promoting her product and her image.

Walker's carefully constructed, widely distributed star image had the effect of creating a unique space from which to address

African Americans. Most often this address urged African American women to join her in the business sphere and to gain a level of economic freedom, and her image modeled the type of success possible for other African Americans. At the same time, the construction and distribution of her image had the effect of reconfiguring the terms of representation for African American women within the public sphere. African American women singled out for representation in mass-produced publications were generally highly educated and concerned with either uplift activities or including African American women within hegemonic ideologies of domesticity. Walker's image served to broaden the possibilities and route an African American woman might take to gain prominence. Indeed, in later years, Walker used her image to position herself in the company of such African American leaders as Booker T. Washington, a strategy that became particularly evident in her use of so-called illustrated lectures.

These illustrated lectures were accompanied by a printed booklet that included an accounting of her real estate holdings and their locations, and a narrative that highlighted Walker's decision to attend business school.[20] Booklets also included articles and press releases about either Walker or her company. Between ten thousand to twenty thousand were printed each month from 1915 until her death in 1919.[21] One of her advertising tools, the illustrated lecture provides an opportunity to look closely at the production of the Walker image in relation to African American leaders and at the way Walker claimed authority for herself while redefining herself and her profession to others.

Illustrated Pictures, Class Conflict, and Black Colleges

An illustrated lecture by Walker amounted to a slide show featuring images of Walker, F. B. Ransom (Walker's attorney), her daughter, A'Lelia, Booker T. Washington, and other African American leaders. The lectures also included images of African

American entrepreneurs and narratives about their businesses. Some slides demonstrated her method of hair care; some depicted her homes, cars, and salons. At times she offered financial advice, asking listeners to support an African American company that she thought was doing a good job, and she would include pictures of the founders of these companies as well as the buildings they owned. The first and last images, however, were always of Madam Walker.

The opening head shot in the slide show would have been easily identifiable to lecture attendees because the company generally flooded the area surrounding the lecture site with advertising for Walker Company products before the presentation. They also tried to distribute a "self-authored" newspaper article that often included a head shot of Walker. Neither these advertisements nor articles offered the full story behind Walker's rise to fortune, but she utilized this format to ensure that listeners were offered the story in a way that was designed to inspire.

After the initial head shot, the viewer saw a photograph of a sharecropper's shack, indicating Walker's lowly birth into a sharecropping family. The next photograph, of an old wooden washtub, allowed her to explain that when she was seven years old, she and her sister began to take in laundry to make ends meet and that she worked as a laundress for thirty years. What followed these two photographs were pictures of her present home and many of her possessions. This strategy underscored the contrast between the simple, "humble" objects with which she began and her present material success. The succession of photos of her material success was followed by pictures of Walker in the company of well-known African American leaders and businesspeople.

Looking closely at the Walker star image, however, one can see that it masked ambivalence about her relationship to the "elite" classes and their relationship to working-class African Americans. These feelings were influenced by her experiences with this group when she was still a laundress. For example, describing the reception she received by the African American community in her hometown of St. Louis, Walker writes, "You should have seen the dictey who did not notice the washerwoman falling on their faces to see her, and everyone wanted to entertain me, but I didn't accept one social call."[22] Here Walker displays a disdain for upper-class African Americans who now are interested in entertaining her, although they wanted nothing to do with her before she was wealthy and well known. Although her celebrity and business success had made her worthy of note, it is she who now refuses to notice this class of African Americans.

In late 1916, dissention broke out at company headquarters because some of the women office workers discovered that those engaged in manual labor at the factory were paid almost twice as much as they were paid. In a letter to F. B. Ransom, Walker writes that this policy is a

> bone of contention between Lucy and me. She contends that Alice should not be paid any more than she because her work was brain work and Alice did the laborious part. I take the stand that laborious work such as done in my factory is worth more than the office work. You would find many persons who have been trained for the office and could fill any one of their places much easier than you could Turner's or Miss Kelly's, for everybody is looking for an easy job.[23]

"Brain work," then, is easier so far as Walker is concerned, and mixing the preparations and packaging the boxes are what she chooses to reward monetarily. This is significant in that it appears to run counter to those ideologies that position education as the more important goal for African Americans. By paying physical laborers more, Walker recognized a class of African Americans who were rarely if ever singled out as exemplary by "New Negro" ideologists and in the process offers what constitutes a critique of such beliefs.

In an often-delivered speech titled "The Negro Woman in Business," Walker told listeners, "Now I realize that in the so-called higher walks of life, many were prone to look down upon hair dressers, as they called us. They didn't have a very high opinion of our calling, so I had to go down and dignify this work, so much that many of the best women of our race are now engaged in this line of business."[24] There is an irony in Walker critiquing the "higher walks of life," given that at the time she addressed these audiences, her business was bringing in approximately $1,000 a week, probably far higher than the income of many of this group's wealthiest members. However, the phrasing of this talk suggests a similarity between Walker and her listeners at the expense of those in the so-called upper class. Indeed, it appears she did not have a very high opinion of this class of African Americans, because she calls into question the veracity of a statement affirming their superiority to working-class African Americans. It is not altogether clear what Walker believed she had done to "dignify" hairdressing as a profession, but it certainly would have included her involvement with black colleges during the period. To "dignify" work that was thought to be performed by a lower class of African American women, Walker maneuvered to have it offered in colleges. She positioned her work in this forum in relation to hegemonic notions of education.

In 1916, Walker began to lay the groundwork for a plan to have her system of hair treatment become a part of the curriculum of colleges that catered primarily to an African American student body. These mostly vocational schools had as their mission educating African Americans in specific skills with which they could earn a living. For women, curriculum choices were limited; they were aimed basically at enhancing teaching and homemaking skills. Walker's plan was designed to make this new course of study beneficial to the individual Walker agents as well as to the educational institution, the African American women students, and the Walker Manufacturing Company.

Under the plan, a duly trained and licensed Walker agent would become a member of the college faculty. She would live at the college without charge and train students in the Walker method of treatment. Walker believed this arrangement would work because women from the surrounding areas could serve as customers and would receive a reduced rate for the services provided by students. If the agent wished to set up a shop in town, she could do so and charge the full price for her services. However, any money made by the agent using students of the college would be divided between the college and the agent. Walker strongly advised that the college open a shop on campus so that it could profit financially from the services of the Walker agent and the students. The preparations for use in the program were to be purchased at the regular price from the company.

To make this proposal more attractive to colleges, Walker offered to donate $100 to construct a room at the institution in which classes would be taught. If the cost of construction ran over that amount, she would make up the difference. She also offered to set up a scholarship fund of $500 to educate African American women in the art of beauty culture. The school was responsible for choosing the student it believed most deserving.

Walker received affirmative responses to this proposal from colleges all over the South, and college presidents who had not received a letter asking them to participate in the program wrote to ask if their schools could be included.[25] By the end of 1917, at least twenty colleges from Florida to Tennessee had accepted the proposal and were offering the Walker method of hair treatment at their institutions.

Walker's excursion into African American colleges is significant on a number of levels. Not only did she make it possible for individual Walker agents to become part of college faculties throughout the South, but she guaranteed that hairdressing would become a viable trade for numbers of African American women. She attempted to underwrite such success by offering scholarships. Women in surrounding communities also benefited by receiving Walker treatments at a reduced rate, and the colleges benefited by having their curricula enhanced and made attractive to many African American women at no cost to themselves. Finally, the Walker Company was assured of product sales as well as new customers and a positive corporate image. Not only had it developed new markets, at a relatively low cost, but it had helped African American women learn a trade and had offered them an option outside of teaching, homemaking, and domestic work for whites.

One woman who learned her trade through this program in an African American college stated, "You have opened up a trade for hundreds of colored women to make an honest and profitable living where they make as much in one week as a month's salary would bring from any other position that a colored woman can secure."[26] Walker's program made it possible for almost any African American woman to join the ranks of the business class and sidestep proscriptions around the meaning of education and its relationship to domesticity. By this time, hairdressing had come of age and was considered a respectable profession that was wholeheartedly supported, if not endorsed, by the African American middle classes.

Madam C. J. Walker was adept at structuring and distributing an image for both herself and her company. Not only did she write self-promotional articles that she convinced various African American newspapers to publish, but she employed agents whose primary job was to enhance her image. Walker's image construction most often contrasted her working-class history with her later wealth, highlighting the advantages of aligning oneself with her business, as well as her importance to the African American community.

At the same time, Walker structured a story that would have been familiar to working-class African American women in a way that pointed out her similarities with and understanding of their position. She told them she had married to lessen her personal and economic hardships, but it had ended in divorce. She had worked at menial labor all her life and taken pride in that hard work, but it had not brought her rewards. Only when she began to work for herself was she was able to gain wealth and respectability within African American communities. As a result, she structured an identity that privileged the amount of money she had and the lavishness with which she spent it. Because she wanted to inspire individuals with the story of her life, she positioned her consumption as a prerequisite for her status as a celebrity or star in African American communities and built off of that construction, becoming an "attraction" and charging others a fee to hear her lecture. Whereas the purpose of her star image was to sell products, its effect was to allow her to address African American communities in a manner that masked her ambivalence about the relationship of hegemonic ideologies of class to working-class African American women.

Walker's specific views about gender relationships, while not specifically articulated in her public discourses, impacted the ways she operated in the world. She did not publicly address the ways she believed African American men and women should relate to each other, but privately she implied that African American women were more reliable and trustworthy than African American men. Rather than taking an anti-male stance, however, Walker positioned herself as pro-woman; while not forbidding men to sell her products or to occupy some positions in her company, she believed that the company was in existence to serve and aid other women.

These actions, however, took place in her "private sphere," to which a majority of African Americans had no access. For example, Walker left instructions in her will that only another woman could become president of her company.[27] She also decreed that the secret formula only be taught to another woman. Both of these positions were to be held by a member of the immediate family, if possible, but if someone from outside the family were to perform these functions, that person had to be a woman. Also, a majority of positions within the company were held by African American women.

Although F. B. Ransom served as Walker's attorney for many years, he too was subject to her views on gender. In 1916, while responding to a letter from Ransom telling her of the birth of a son, Walker wrote, "I can't say that I congratulate you because I am disgusted that you have so many boys. Ha Ha." While

Walker was clearly joking with a long-trusted friend, these views do not seem very different from what she believed. Perhaps even more telling are the ways these views were taken up by the groups of women Walker addressed and, in some instances, was responsible for organizing.

Walker's concerns surrounding class, gender, and the role of the elite professional classes within African American communities forced her to remake herself in her own image. That is, she could not draw on ideologies that privileged education and middle-class notions of domesticity because her life did not include these things. As a result, she reconfigured the terms of the debate to include characteristics she did possess—money and a Protestant work ethic. She invited other African American women to join her in this process of reconfiguration, and a new understanding of the possibility for and meaning of hair was born. The midwife at the rebirth was *Woman's Voice* magazine.

5

Gender, Hair, and African American Women's Magazines

This chapter is not so much about hair's significance as it is about the opportunities hairdressing afforded a group of African American women to address the tensions that working outside of the home caused in individual African American households. Although Madam C. J. Walker was instrumental in "dignifying" hairdressing as a career, the familial issues involved in working outside of the home created turmoil that hairdressers, at least, thought needed to be addressed. A new magazine, *Woman's Voice,* came along to map out the problem and offer advice to readers about the changes that had to take place in family relationships as a result of these new roles.

While planning the first national conference of Walker agents, held in Philadelphia in 1917, members of the Madam C. J. Walker Hair Culturists Union of Philadelphia worked with local members of the Madam C. J. Walker clubs to put together a conference program, which they termed an "advertising matter." Margaret Thompson, president of the Walker Hair Culturists Union, writing to F. B. Ransom, called the conference program "the most unique publication ever run in this city. It is souvenir and historic combined. It is about the size of the *Literary Digest* and contains 20 pages of history and advertisement of Negro-business mainly women in the city."[1] This souvenir program was a big success at the convention, and union and club members approached Walker about publishing it regularly. She agreed and *Woman's Voice* was born.

When I first learned of the magazine, I hoped it would reflect the psyches of African American hairdressers. That is, I hoped it was an arena for hairdressers to discuss in print the thoughts and perspectives I remember hearing while a patron at the beauty shop. Although I do not think *Woman's Voice* was an unmediated site of working-class women's interests and desires, as a publication backed by and marketed to hairdressers, it offers interesting insights. In much the same way that *Essence* magazine is marketed as the place to go to discern the desires and identities of successful African American women, the publisher and editor of *Woman's Voice* saw themselves performing a similar function for working-class African American women in the early twentieth century.

Woman's Voice is exemplary in that it portrays an identity for African American women that contested and (re)presented constructions and representations of African American women's bodies within African American communities and ideologies. At the same time, these representations are substantially similar to concerns Walker addressed. As a result, *Woman's Voice* illustrates the ways that Walker's views of African American women's identities were shared by a larger group of African American women editors, writers, and readers.

Periodicals have often been discussed as a primary location for studying the expanding role of women's participation in mass culture as readers, writers, and textual figures. Kathryn Shevelow goes so far as to argue that early periodicals are a principal site for the normative construction of femininity in writing because they function as public disseminators of prescriptions for private behavior. Thus, magazines produced by

African American women can be useful for discerning the ways these women "constructed for public consumption, normative images of 'private life.' "[2]

These constructions were important because of the conflicting representations of African American identity that were being marketed; many were aimed especially at African Americans newly migrated from the South. Indeed, some have argued that African American editors and writers in northern periodicals saw a large part of their task as setting and defining the terms of citizenship for this new group of immigrants.[3] As a result, competing ideologies of racial identity based on class and gender proscriptions were packaged and sold, and magazines were a key site for their construction.

During the height of migration, roughly 1910 through 1920, northern cities such as Chicago already had a sizable African American population. For example, Nicholas Lemann reports that in 1910, there were 44,000 African Americans in Chicago, and that by 1920, the number had increased to 109,000.[4] Many of the earlier migrants identified themselves as middle class and constructed representations that portrayed themselves as educated, refined, and forward thinking. Newer migrants, however, were often discussed and spoken to as if they were lower class and therefore uncivilized or lacking the basic skills needed to be considered upstanding members of "The Race." This treatment had particular implications for African American women.

Hazel Carby has argued that the migration of working-class African American women from rural to urban areas facilitated a number of "moral panics" by the middle class. Focusing on various discourses and the way they positioned the sexual behavior of migrating women as a threat to stable communities in the North, Carby argues that migrating women were portrayed as a danger to social order. Carby sets up a paradigm within which the African American middle classes function as a buffer between the dominant culture and a working-class population. Through the middle class, many of the judgments surrounding morality and civilized behavior are placed in a specifically

African American context and communicated to a working class or underclass. This focus on "proper behavior" then became a prerequisite for middle-class status in African American communities.[5]

This reasoning implies that the African American middle class was homogeneous and that the terms for acceptance by middle-class African Americans were actually a complete ideology represented uproblematically within the discourses of various novels and periodicals. This was not the case. Indeed, even within two periodicals published by and marketed for African American women—*Half-Century Magazine* and *Woman's Voice*—there are ideological clashes and differing proscriptions for African American women's place within their communities.

Half-Century Magazine (1916–1925) and *Woman's Voice* (1917–1948) lend themselves to comparison. Although one had a much longer life span than the other, each was published and edited by African American women in large northern, urban cities with significant African American populations. Both constructed audiences who were primarily female, married, and with children, and both were underwritten by large cosmetic manufacturing concerns. Whereas the construction of female readers as located largely within the "home" certainly reinscribes ideas about domesticity found in dominant culture, it is significant that this stance was marketed to an African American female population that worked outside the home.[6] However, the meanings of "wife," "mother," and indeed "domesticity," as discussed in these two publications, differ significantly.[7]

Whereas *Woman's Voice* assumes women want a life outside the home, *Half-Century Magazine* positions women in relationship to the domestic sphere and teaches them to perform basic tasks within the home. One teaches the finer points of domesticity, and the other offers advice on how to be in business, have a family, and prioritize personal time. Thus, *Half-Century Magazine* represents gender identity unproblematically and home as an idealized space.

Half-Century Magazine

Published from 1916 through 1925, *Half-Century Magazine* took its name from the fifty years that had passed since emancipation. The owner, publisher, and editor-in-chief from 1916 to 1918 is listed in financial records as Katherine Williams. After 1918, she is only one of five owners listed, but she continued to publish and edit the magazine. Early issues were approximately twenty pages in length, with roughly one-third of the publication taken up by advertisements. The remainder comprised short fiction, biographical sketches, serialized novels, editorials, and columns discussing the importance of business and/or "women's issues." Reliable circulation figures are impossible to obtain, although some have estimated that they reached as high as 16,000.[8]

In the premier issue, the editor is careful to position the magazine against other so-called race publications and to identify an ideological stance for readers. She states that the magazine will publish articles about African Americans who have achieved prominence, because the editors believe this will be of interest to the majority of their readers. However, she is clear that they will refrain from publishing articles that would be of interest only to those individuals who are mentioned by name, as "such news items are fully covered by our leading Colored weeklies, [and] we leave the field to their complete monopolistic control."

As the editor makes a case for the need of her publication, she exhibits a fair amount of disdain toward what she terms "Colored weeklies" that report news about which the majority of African Americans are uninterested. Indeed, in positioning *Half-Century* against African American weekly periodicals, Williams makes it clear that she sees the ideology and content of her magazine as significantly different, if not superior. Williams then outlines the philosophy that will guide further issues of the magazine. She believes that while the "Race Problem" should be discussed, African Americans must begin to acknowledge that they are living in a "commercial era and that the factors of paramount importance in the solution of this problem are economy, industry—the making and saving of money—and business development."[9] She goes on to add that unity, cooperation, and race patronage are essential for any advancement by African Americans as a whole.

This opening editorial gives prospective readers a clear understanding of why the editor believes the magazine is important and different from other African American publications. The magazine will emphasize the business and financial strategies necessary to solve the problems African Americans face, highlighting African Americans who are successful in business as well as offering advice on how others may follow in their footsteps. This rational is reminiscent of W.E.B. Du Bois's call for the "talented tenth" of African Americans to lead the other 90 percent out of ignorance and despair. While Du Bois's tenth was concerned mainly with literary and scholarly achievements, the publisher of *Half-Century* suggests that this type of leadership needs to come from businesspeople. In any case, the editor opposes ideologies for solving African Americans' problems that do not have a central focus on economics.

From 1916 to 1918, the magazine was subtitled the *Colored Monthly for the Business Man and the Home Maker.* As the title implies, business is discussed solely in relation to African American men; home is the place for women, who are "home makers." Men and women are rarely if ever spoken to about the same interests. It is significant then that, after a few years, the magazine reduced its size and cost, dropped much of its emphasis on business, and labeled itself *A Colored Magazine for the Home and Home Maker.*[10] This name change signaled a shift to focus solely on women, a change that may have been due to the readership's lack of interest in businessmen or ideologies that positioned business as a solution to African American problems. Interest in constructions of African American women within the domestic sphere clearly maintained a significant amount of cultural currency, and the magazine began to function as a handbook for social and hygienic do's and don't's. As a result, it underscores Carby's contention that the African American middle classes were particularly concerned with "civilizing" newly migrated women. These concerns are most aptly illustrated in the four monthly columns titled "Beauty Hints," "Domestic Science," "Fashions," and "Etiquette."

"Beauty Hints" discusses the relationship of personal hygiene to larger beauty constructs. Topics in this column range from the necessity for brushing one's teeth, clipping one's nails, and taking baths and the importance of cleanliness for maintaining healthy skin. Interestingly enough, the skin color of African American women is rarely if ever mentioned, and hair texture is almost never addressed except to offer advice on how to keep hair clean. For example, in the column "The Care of the Hair," the author states that "modern specialists" have discovered that washing the hair once a month, or every six weeks, is "no less unhygienic than the 'Saturday Night' bath." She goes on to ask, "Why should we expect our hair to keep cleaner than any other part of the body. . . . Modern practice teaches us that dry hair should be shampooed once every two weeks and oily hair may be washed thoroughly every week." The column ends with instructions to the reader on the way to use shampoo and how to rinse the hair to make sure it is thoroughly cleaned.[11]

This almost step-by-step guide to hair washing is coupled with an article in the "Domestic Science" column, entitled "What to Eat and How to Cook It," instructing African American women on the procedure for selecting beef from the butcher. Like the article on hair washing, it offers a step-by-step guide: at home, the meat "should be removed from the paper as soon as it arrives from the market and put in a cold place. If convenient, allow it to hang rather than to lie on a plate and never put it in direct contact with the ice." Following these admonishments are several recipes for cooking the steak. These types of articles suggest that the writers see themselves as having to instruct African American women, at the most basic level, about the most mundane tasks. They appear to be speaking to persons not used to practicing "good" hygiene and "modern" cooking techniques.

Half-Century also offered advice on the finer points of social etiquette. The magazine included columns for women concerned with "proper" etiquette when "coming to call" on friends and acquaintances, as well as procedures for planning large weddings and hiring competent "help." By publishing such radically different columns, the editors seem to include women of different classes. That is, women who are interested in such finer points of etiquette as what to wear, what times to call, what type of calling cards to have printed up, and what food to serve guests would not have been among the same population who had no idea what a stove was or how to shampoo the hair. Clearly the magazine saw itself as speaking in one voice to its middle-class constituents and, at the same time, speaking in another to those they believed needed basic instruction on life in the North. In both cases, however, women are positioned within the home, and all of the instruction contained in the magazine attempts to teach them the best, most socially "acceptable" practices in that sphere.

In portraying the home as a place most befitting African American women, *Half-Century* rarely, if ever, discussed interpersonal relationships between men and women and made little effort to critique class and gender expectations in American and/or African American culture. Rather, it reinscribed the dominant positions in its pages. As a result, *Half-Century* constituted a narrower ideological leaning, which placed the publication on a distinct side of the debate about women's place and what women needed to prosper.

Half-Century's representations of African American women contrast with those found in *Woman's Voice*; the latter shows a broader range of identities both constructed and represented and a challenging of desire for obtaining middle-class status as constituted by the focus on "proper" behavior for women. Within *Woman's Voice,* constructs of class and gender were prioritized in ways that produced oppositional discourses and representations.

Woman's Voice

Early in 1916, Madam C. J. Walker began considering purchase of a magazine in which her friend and sometime business partner Louis George and her financial adviser Arthur Singerman were interested.[12] Although this proposed venture was not acted on, Walker set out her motivation for undertaking such a project. She believed the magazine would serve as a mouthpiece for the Walker Company in general and her agents in particular. She grounded her reasoning on a desire to further promote race literature and to provide her women employees with a means of voicing their opinions and concerns regarding American culture. Also, she saw an opportunity to diversify her business holdings:

> As you know, the way with most Negro Magazines is you are never able to depend on them for they haven't sufficient capital behind them to keep it before the public until it begins making money. I thought should I take it on I would set up a printing establishment which would not only be able to get out the magazine, but would do a great deal of job printing and all of my own literature which amounts to several thousand dollars per year.[13]

Probably these same concerns led her to agree to finance *Woman's Voice* magazine. In describing *Woman's Voice,* the advertising department sent out mailers urging women not only to read the publication but to enter a contest to promote subscriptions. One mailer informed agents:

> *Woman's Voice* is a splendid colored woman's magazine, in fact the only such magazine on the market today. . . . It is a colored journal written and printed for and by colored people. Go out, tell your friends, your acquaintances and the public generally of the large amount of live news, good stories, humorous opinion

> and the wealth of pictures, all contained in each and every copy
> of the Voice. . . . It is not a new magazine, but is 80 months old,
> well read and widely circulated and it is backed by sufficient
> capital to insure its continuous and consecutive monthly
> appearance.[14]

Although actual circulation figures are difficult to ascertain, it appears from financial records that in 1920 and 1921, the company paid to have five thousand copies printed each month. The editor of the publication estimated that each copy actually purchased was read by between two and five persons.[15]

The origins of Walker's relationship with Sommerville V. Fauntleroy, the first "editress" (as she was listed on the masthead), is unknown, but from articles published in the magazine, we know that Fauntleroy was a speaker at the yearly conventions of Walker agents, beginning in 1919, and that she spoke every year through 1937. She urged conference attendees to read the magazine to learn more about African American women's history and current political activities and to use the publication to advertise their services as beauty culturists.[16] Indeed, most of the magazine's advertisements came from practitioners of Walker's beauty process and detailed Walker's accomplishments as well as those of the company and her immediate family. In the July 1922 issue, an italicized message to readers at the bottom of every third page urges attendance at the Walker agents' convention in August of that year.

Of the approximately twenty to thirty pages per issue, there were usually two to three long articles, which were often written as editorials. A number of biographical sketches of African American women, and, occasionally, African American men, were also included. In many of the issues was a section that discussed people of African descent in Europe, the Caribbean, South America, or Africa. Finally, a "Current News" section gave brief synopses of worldwide events affecting African Americans. Although there was never much poetry or fiction published (there were two poems in all the issues I looked at), in later years the editors added a "Book Chat" that reviewed works dealing with African Americans in the Diaspora.

The front cover featured either a "nature" scene or a photograph of an African American woman. At times this photograph was of a celebrity, such as Florence Mills, Bessie Smith, or Madam C. J. Walker herself; just as often, the woman was someone known in various local communities for her "service." In the bottom right-hand corner of each cover was a circle with the inscription "For women, By women, Of women." There was no mention of race in either the title or the magazine's motto.

Ellen McCracken has argued that the cover is a magazine's most important advertisement because it is the label or packaging that helps readers decide to purchase one magazine over another. She adds, "Together, the visual images and headlines on a magazine cover offer a complex semiotic system, communicating primary and secondary meanings through language, photographs, images, color and placement."[17] Given that the Walker Company saw this publication as aimed at an African American audience, their choice to exclude race from both the title and the motto constitutes such an ideological stance. Rather than proclaim *Woman's Voice* as a publication for an African American female "other," they sought to include African American women in the category of "woman." In so doing, they reconfigured "womanhood" as a term inclusive of African American women. Race is reinserted, however, by use of a photograph of an African American woman on a majority of the covers.

The inscription on the first page of each issue provides a clear insight into the purpose of the publication and signals the breadth of topics in which African American women might or should be interested. It states: this is "a monthly Magazine through which woman can express her Hopes, Ideas, Ideals. Interested in Spiritual, Educational, Social, Domestic, Political, Financial and Business Achievements. A magazine that gives you Food for Thought." Instead of addressing women in the context of the home, *Woman's Voice* was aimed at an audience interested in business, politics, and various ideas regarding these constructs, as well as the home.

Woman's Voice did not subscribe to the rigid gender defini-

tions prevalent in *Half-Century Magazine*. Differences in ideologies are especially evident in the articles and editorials that
utilize direct address to speak to African American men. In
Woman's Voice, the majority of articles that address men offer
them advice on how to be a more supportive partner/husband/
father and housekeeper, although a number of editorials instruct men on how to be better persons in their business deal-
ings and in their relationships with other men.[18] Sometimes
Woman's Voice cautioned women readers that men were con-
tradictory if not impossible to understand.

· For example, in an inversion of the age-old adage regarding
women's incomprehensibility to men, one writer asks, "Who
Can Guess a Man."[19] Here the unnamed writer questions the
reasoning ability of men. Among other observations, the writer
points out that "He considers that no woman has a right to
expect her husband to be romantically in love with her after she
gets fat, and grizzle-headed, but he expects to remain the hero of
his wife's girlish dreams no matter how bald and bay win-
dowed he becomes." She goes on to say that "He derides a
woman's logic, but adopts her conclusions" and that "In theory,
he admires a woman who is sensible and self controlled, but he
marries the little goose who weeps on the second button of his
waistcoat."

Here the double standard regarding the responsibilities of
men and women in a relationship or marriage are critiqued, and
the writer suggests that the rules should be changed. What is
significant, however, is the way she positions men as the ones
who need to change. By placing that responsibility on African
American men, the article addresses them within the context of
domestic ideology in a way that challenges their abrogation of
responsibility for the emotional well-being of their wives. These
views about men and their relationships to women are strikingly different from those expressed in *Half-Century.* Whereas
Half-Century chose to address men only within the business
field, *Woman's Voice* repositions them within the home and,
most importantly, in relationship to women.

In another article entitled "Mere Man or Mere Woman?" the

editor addresses relationships between men and women outside of the home and begins by asking if men and women can
work together in political groups. In responding to the sugges-
tion by an unnamed politician that the National Association for
the Advancement of Colored People (NAACP) would be more
effective if men and women had separate branches, the writer
says that on the surface, more seems to be accomplished when
the sexes work separately, as in men's lodges and women's
clubs. She goes on to say that it is amazing that men and women
get along as well as they do within families, when one considers
the ways men attempt to control women at every turn: "There
seems to be something in masculine make up that says always 'I
am the head.' And this is not to discredit man's ability, either,
but to emphasize that there is truth in the assertion that the
sexes do not co-operate in joint efforts to the best advantages."[20]

While the editor and writers for *Woman's Voice* acknowledged
the presence of men in their readers' lives, they warned women
against regarding men and children as the center. Urging
women to fashion an identity for themselves before joining in a
relationship with a man, writers often questioned the practice of
pursuing men to obtain marriage and respectability. One article
goes so far as to suggest that these attitudes are akin to those
that forced some African American women into prostitution. In
a December 1921 volume, under a column entitled "Helping
One Another," is an article, "The Only Way to Hold a Man," that
juxtaposes the attitudes of a neighborhood prostitute named
Maymee, a "nice" working girl named Ella, and a wealthy single woman named Constance. All three are said to be preoc-
cupied with makeup, clothes, body size, and attentiveness to
male sexual desire in hopes of attracting a man to take care of
them and give them a sense of respectability.[21]

This writer pays special attention to the ways that women
from different classes position themselves as superior to those
"below" them and shows that the logic the three women use to
justify their behavior is flawed. For example, Maymee says that
she spends so much time dressing and making up for men
because "the men won't look at you unless you do." Ella, who

works at a department store in the notions section, has her eye on a young man who works at the same store. Ella says she wouldn't behave in the same way Maymee does, even if it meant she had to earn her own living for the rest of her life. She does, however, wear her hair in a style that her young man likes, buys clothes and lingerie of which he approves, and shaves her eyebrows because "You can't get 'em any other way."

In describing Constance, the writer states that "Her hair is ever so delicately hennaed, her skin tinted and her figure modeled by the most expert hands. The upkeep of Constance's beauty amounts to a small fortune but 'it's the only way to hold a man.'" The writer says that Constance feels that women like Ella and Maymee are "crude, vulgar things," and she is happy that, because she lives in an exclusive part of town, she does not have to come into contact with them. This is one of the reasons she is anxious to marry "young Deekford who can buy Constance half a dozen chateaux if she pleases him sufficiently—and Constance sees to it that she pleases him."

This article positions women's sexuality as a commodity that will buy them comfort and, in their minds, respectability. This point is underlined by the final paragraph, which states, "So on we go, yammering at the sinfulness of Maymee, and the stillness of Ella, yet never do we see that they are the products of the identically the same vicious idea which clothes Constance in gowns from Chanel and Miler Soeurs and the mantle of respectability." Respectability, as constituted by class position, is critiqued as problematic for women because it may be had only by pleasing men. By drawing comparisons between a woman who earns her living through sexual intercourse with men and a wealthy society woman who hopes to maintain her position in the same manner, the writer suggests that there are more similarities than differences between the two women.

The article's ending, however, criticizes society for its role in attacking women from a lower class than Constance instead of dismantling the patriarchy, which, the article suggests, oppresses all women. As a result, ideologies within African American communities that seek to position women's identities only in relationship to class and marital status are critiqued, and the "vicious idea" that adherence to hegemonic constructs by members of different classes will bring reward is challenged.

The majority of the articles in *Woman's Voice* address women as if they are in a relationship with a man and have a family. However, instead of concentrating on the ways one may become more firmly entrenched within the domestic sphere, these articles offer women advice for maintaining their own identity within the institution of marriage and caution against becoming what the magazine frequently terms "A Back Number." The editors include laments for African American women who have attempted to live up to the societal prescription of motherhood (oftentimes referred to as slavery), only to find that real life (constructed as the public sphere) has passed them by.

For example, in an article entitled "Back Numbers," the writer begins by telling readers that there is a "great deal of complaint" regarding women spending time in the home as opposed to in "the whirlpool of life." Although the writer is not sure if "the new freedom" will be an "absolute 'fit' or a 'misfit,'" she argues,

> We have the clinging-vine type of mother and we shall always have her, for the forces that go into her making are ever present. She does what she is told after the fashion of the child. She minds when she is spoken to by her lord and master. She takes no thought of the morrow for she knows that her strong man is going to do that for her. Her mind today is just where it was when John was born twenty years ago. Women all about her have completely changed places with their former selves and the clinging-vine-woman never discovered that anything was going on.[22]

While the "clinging vine" type of mother is described as concerned with maintaining patriarchy by remaining in the domestic sphere, the article goes on to say that

> It is possible for a woman to spend all the time necessary with her family and yet get away from it long enough to recognize that distance lends enchantment. She is entitled by every right

> of motherhood to go on an occasional vacation, to go to her
> club and to the political meetings. It is all right if she asks father
> to stay home. . . . Let the women be mothers and wives in the
> completest sense of the terms and let them be Women!

The writer of this article does not suggest that wives and mothers should forsake their families in pursuit of personal development and interests. She does, however, critique certain behaviors adhered to by men and women within the confines of the home. Women who allow themselves to be treated as children and give no thought to the world outside of the home are challenged to construct a definition of motherhood that subverts the centrality of the domestic sphere. Indeed, the author argues that societal definitions of womanhood that do not acknowledge the necessity for women to engage in personal activities must be stretched to allow women time for themselves and their issues. As a result, she suggests that "women" is a term capable of encompassing far more than it usually denotes.

Although the writer begins this article by saying she will look at two sides of the argument surrounding "women's place," she comes down clearly on the side of women taking an active interest in politics and the world outside the family. Although she spends considerable space sneering at women who are content to be "back numbers," the writer places the responsibility for the existence of such women on forces outside of the control of individual women. As a result, this article is a call for women to resist hegemonic constructions of their identities, which deny them agency and reinforce patriarchy. Here the magazine appears to espouse the beliefs of "domestic feminism," the view that there is no incompatibility between women's domestic and professional roles and that women should work in the domestic sphere to "upgrade the morality of the home and family" and in the public sphere to bring about needed reforms.[23]

Domestic feminism and the type of women who lived that ideal are illustrated in the biographical sketches in *Woman's Voice*, which functioned to give African American women role models. All the sketches highlight women who had husbands and children but also were successful in business or political work. In one sketch, entitled "Mrs. Maggie Lena Walker— Superwoman," the writer begins, "To say that Mrs. Walker has done a man's work, merely because she has done a number of things usually done by men, is not a fair statement of the case, rather she has done her own work in her own way" (7). Maggie Lena Walker was one of the few women bank presidents and the only African American woman to claim the honor. The writer of this sketch is careful to point out that Walker is a "family" woman who has found a way to make time for her work and family, as well as be active in the church and in politics.

In a sketch of the life of Mary Townsend Seymour, the writer begins by saying, "A chilling inconsistency is inflicted upon the aspirations of young girls to whom most examples of feminine leadership are presented. For while picturing the reward of work, patience, and the usual qualities that in the end win out yet they most frequently point to the abnormal lives which say by implication that only those women who forgo family and home life are eligible for greatness" (10). The writer takes care to point out that a life without a home and family is an unacceptable alternative for most women, which is why she has chosen to look at this particular woman's life. Seymour began her life of activism when she organized against legislation aimed at "consigning colored women in the South to the political insignificance of colored men." However, at the same time she was able to raise children and have a husband.

In its pages, *Woman's Voice* offered a wider range of African American female identity than was offered elsewhere, and there was a constant process of (re)inscription, subversion, and resistance at work. At times, articles encourage women to attempt to fashion an identity wholly separate from the domestic sphere; other times, they suggest that African American women should try to balance the two. As a result, African American women attempting to follow the magazine's prescriptions were offered various choices. However, *Woman's Voice*, like many mass-produced women's magazines, offered "representations of

women which are either downright reactionary, or at least subtly maintain sexual difference and women's subordination."24

Although the writers posited strategies for negotiating class
and gender proscriptions and critiques of African American
women's place within African American culture, they did so in
a manner that maintained sexual difference. That is to say, with
some notable exclusions, the writers were careful to address
women as if they were in a relationship with a man and as if
some type of domestic responsibility would fall on their
shoulders. However, in positioning the domestic sphere as opposed to a public one, the magazine urged its readers to
broaden the definition of what should occur in the home. As a
result, it championed the accomplishments of middle-class
"superwomen" who juggled family responsibilities along with
politics and business. The magazine, therefore, argued for construction of an African American female identity that focused
substantially on the public sphere.

These representations are consistent with the ideas that
Walker espoused, in her interviews and speeches, regarding
African American women's relation to the public sphere.
Whereas Walker's speeches and advertisements lend insight
into the ways she contested hegemonic ideals surrounding African American female identity, the magazine allowed room for
exploring the particulars of negotiating and, in some cases,
straddling public and private personas. Perhaps because
Woman's Voice was begun by a group of working-class African
American women who earned their living as hairdressers, or
because they marketed the publication to and through those
same women, the editors and writers of *Woman's Voice* were
able to problematize as well as critique gender conventions and
offer broader alternatives. In any case, the publication they produced functioned as a voice for representations and identities of
African American women that were significantly different from
those offered elsewhere.

6

In Search of Connections

There are three major circles of reality in American society, which reflect degrees of power and powerlessness. There is a large circle in which white people, most of them men, experience influence and power. Far away from it there is a smaller circle, a narrow space, in which black people, regardless of sex, experience uncertainty, exploitation, and powerlessness. Hidden in this second circle is a third, a small, dark enclosure in which black women experience pain, isolation, and vulnerability. These are the distinguishing marks of black womanhood in white America.
—Gloria Wade-Gayles, *No Crystal Stair*

Before you can read me, you've got to learn how to see me.
—"Free Your Mind," En Vogue

Gloria Wade-Gayles is one of my favorite writers. Her remembrances and images often touch my unspoken longings, desires, and understandings. Her words quoted in the epigraph are ones I feel deeply whenever I read them. I think it is the circularity of the quotation that is most significant for me: there is no beginning or end, just quixotic movement that cannot help but bring those trapped inside this paradigm back to the start. The circles she describes always appear in my imagination as some sort of polished metal, shining beautifully but impossible to break—connecting and intersecting, but in the end untouched by the efforts of those trapped inside.

In this chapter, I search for intersections, paradigms, and connections with hair politics in more contemporary times. This project, started in the past, now returns to the present and asks if, as we move into the future, we are still trapped inside the same types of beautiful rings Wade-Gayles describes. In many ways, there are more questions here than answers. It all depends on how we choose to "read" what we "see."

The women discussed in these chapters began a debate and set up a paradigm within which hair has come to be understood. They wove a tangled web of significance whose strands included their relationship with their communities and with the larger society, as well as economic considerations and political ideologies. Are current hair politics and discourses substantially similar? Has the meaning and/or cultural significance of hair changed over time? On what or whose terms do contemporary cultural producers address African American women about the significance of their hair? The following anecdotes and incidents seem telling to me, although I am unsure what they say ultimately.

Contemporary Hair Politics

In 1990, black feminist filmmaker Julie Dash released *Daughters of the Dust*. Over the next few years, in widespread acknowledgment of her truly revolutionary portrayal in cinema of African American female identity and culture, the film received no less than thirteen awards. It was praised for its beauty, use of dual narration, multiple point-of-view camera work, comprehensive Afrocentric visual aesthetic, and richness of period detail. Cultural critic Greg Tate pronounced *Daughters* "a film of visionary power conceived with a passion for research." Writer and critic Toni Cade Bambara dubbed the movie "oppositional Africentric cinema." However, one African American female movie reviewer, in defending her reasons for criticizing the film, sniped, "but it's all about hair." In her response, Dash suggested that reducing her work to hair and its significance in African American women's lives was not too far-fetched: "there's a lot of drama around Black hair. . . . I could try to be a filmmaker who was myopic about it, like this really isn't an issue, but that would be untrue."[1]

What is at stake in this little drama about the interpretation of *Daughters of the Dust* is a struggle over the meaning of African American women's identities as constituted by the cultural significance of their hair. Whereas hair meant very different things to the reviewer and the filmmaker, it was central to both. Just as early beauty advertisers marketed understandings of hair in relation to various racial and social ideologies, these two African American women reacted to opposing meanings of hair's significance. What were their precise understandings of hair's importance? I don't know. Are their differing perceptions important? I believe so.

In 1992 in the United States, according to cosmetic industry publications, African Americans represented 19 percent of the toiletries and cosmetics market and, at the same time, bought 34 percent of all hair-care products sold. These figures indicate that African Americans spent three times more than other consumer groups on cosmetics, toiletries, and other grooming needs. Cosmetic industry publications further state that in 1992, the market for hair-care products in the United States was just over $3.9 billion, up 2.8 percent from 1991.[2] In short, African Americans spent a considerable amount of money on hair-care products, the majority of which were designed to straighten our hair. This is a tide that African American activists and intellectuals have attempted to stem since the mid-nineteenth century. Back then, writers such as Booker T. Washington and Nannie Burroughs suggested that if the images of African Americans found in popular culture were changed, or at least were produced by other African Americans, then we would not opt for straight hair. Others believed that a cultural movement aimed at increasing African Americans' love of self was the answer. Since that

time, we have experienced a number of cultural awareness/
self-love movements, and our culture is rich with images created by African Americans. And still we straighten.

Women often change their appearance according to fashion,
but for African American women, texture has become an important expression of identity. What I am most interested in here are
the ways that contemporary hair-care products manufacturers
tap into long-held obsessions with long, straight hair in ways
that speak to African American women. I am also interested in
finding out if marketing strategies involving issues of kinship,
economic self-sufficiency, and alternative body images and
types, prevalent in advertisements at the turn of the century, are
still the stuff of contemporary hair-care advertisements. A recent episode involving a new product for straightening African
American hair provides some insight into these questions.

Early in 1994, late-night television watchers tuned in to a
commercial that promoted a method of hair care for African
Americans. The product, named Rio, was said to have been
used successfully for over forty years by Brazilians who wanted
to straighten their hair. Marketed almost exclusively for sale to
African Americans, Rio promised, in a thirty-minute infomercial, that it would add unforgettable bounce and luster to a
woman's hair. Furthermore, viewers were told that the product
was totally "chemical free." To prove the product's benign ingredients, the male spokesperson actually ate a portion of it on
the air.

Instead of providing soft, flowing hair, however, Rio caused
many users' scalps to itch and burn, while others said it took out
their hair in clumps, leaving embarrassing bald spots. By April
1995, more than fifteen hundred lawsuits had been filed and
attorneys were considering consolidating them into one class
action suit.[3] There is, however, no way to estimate the number
of women who may have suffered ill effects but chose not to
become involved in litigation. The U.S. Food and Drug Admin-
istration locked the company's doors and halted sales.

Some of the women who had negative experiences with the

product say the change in their physical appearance led to social, psychological, and even physical problems. "My attitude is really bad," said Linda Wilkerson, who described her hair as looking like "rats have been sucking on it. I don't even try to fix my hair anymore. It doesn't do any good." Wilkerson added that she was "scared to trust anybody" since she used Rio. Her doctor told her that "my nerves are bad and I have stress ulcers" in the mouth. Another user, Tonya Henderson, said she was a part-time model but that she had done little modeling since huge chunks of her hair fell out and the rest became difficult to style. "Your hair, that's you," Henderson said. "Your hair makes you. I'm basically sad, mad, and hurt because I trusted someone's advertisement. I feel like I've been robbed."[4]

Arthur Rieman, general counsel for World Rio Corporation in Los Angeles, said the company was not to blame for any suffering Rio users might be experiencing and that it would aggressively fight all lawsuits. He went on to add that "It's pretty clear to us that the people who have problems with Rio didn't follow the instructions properly. I wouldn't call people smart or stupid. I don't know why people misuse the product. I don't get it."[5] Given the number of hair-care products currently on the market that are designed to straighten African American hair, it is puzzling that many African American women would purchase this particular product, sight unseen, through the mail. Indeed, the infomercial was the only form of marketing that the company undertook. Therefore, it appears that the message and structure of the advertisement were quite convincing or, at the very least, spoke to African American women's concerns about their hair and its texture.

Beauty advertisements at the turn of the century made explicit claims regarding the necessity of obtaining straight hair and its relation to social and economic advancement. The advertisements relied heavily on "before" and "after" photographs that promised to change African American women from beasts into close approximations of white women, or beauties. There are a number of telling similarities between early mail-order advertisements and the structure and message of Rio. Rio's advertisement relied heavily on the rhetoric of "before" and "after" and on a rationale that made the texture of one's hair the primary basis for achieving fulfillment in life. Here, however, the definition of fulfillment was predicated on being sexually desired by African American men, who, the infomercial told us, only desire women with straight hair that moves.

Rio Hair: The Promise, the Politics

The infomercial's set design evokes visions of a Caribbean resort, and audience members are seated in groups of three or four, at tables made of rattan and bamboo. Large palm trees and numerous "colorful" plants give the appearance of an exotic tropical locale, and a long, large structure in the middle of the set resembles a beach bar. The theme music sounds distinctly like steel drums and does indeed have a "rocking" calypso beat. The spokesman who joins Mary, the model and spokeswoman for Rio, is dressed in a tropical shirt. Mary is dressed in a red, skintight sundress. The set suggests informality. There is no pressure here. We are all relaxed and friendly.

This calm is quickly shattered within the first few moments, as Mary begins to hold a type of pep rally for Rio. "You're going to feel this product," she yells, while pacing back and forth in front of the bar. "You're going to feel it inside you. You're going to feel my hair. I am going to convert every single one of you," she screams, while pumping her fist in the air. "You are going to be chemical free." The earlier, old-fashioned belief that one should straighten one's hair to be free from markers of African ancestry has been replaced with a call for freedom from chemicals. Mary goes on to tell viewers that they have the right to purchase a product that will allow them to be free—to have hair that moves freely when they shake their head.

Mary urges the audience to show their desire for such a product by chanting: "Rio, Rio, Rio." Once the chanting dies down, she shakes her head vigorously to demonstrate what Rio's pur-

Fig. 9. Mary shakes her head.

chasers will gain (fig. 9). Mary then introduces André Desmond, who tells us that he has traveled the world and feels it is his duty to introduce African Americans to the first natural hair-care system that actually works and will allow users to wake up with hair that is "ready to wear." He goes on to warn viewers that the type of hair Rio offers will foster a deep-seated need on the part of African American men to touch such hair. These same men will then ask the hair owners if they can take them out and buy them gifts. He asks Mary to shake her hair again.

At one point, Desmond tells us that "Rio frees you. It doesn't put you in bondage. With Rio you are free." However, as in early beauty advertisements, the freedom he offers may be had only by changing the hair's texture. Hair that is not straight and does not move is not free, and the product Desmond sells has nothing to offer users who wish to wear their hair in its natural state. In addition, African American woman who choose not to purchase this product will apparently suffer from touch deprivation, because there is no possibility of sexual fulfillment without

Figs. 10 and 11. I had bad hair.

changing the texture of the hair. These notions are underscored by the taped testimonials included in the infomercial.

In the first testimonial, a large-boned, dark-skinned woman confides, "I hate my hair, it doesn't move at all. I just wake up in the morning and put on a hat." She tells us, however, that the product is good because it worked on her "bad" hair." A second woman tells us that her hair was so broken off, uneven, and short that it was "just horrible." After using Rio, however, her hair has become moveable, bouncy, full, and manageable (figs. 10 and 11). The one male user tells us that he too just put on a hat in the morning because his hair was such an embarrassment to him, but now "It feels like it's natural. It's awesome " (figs. 12 and 13). The marketers can find little to say that is positive about hair that is not straight and does not move.

Other testimony affirms the advantages of increased male attention by telling viewers that "When my man saw my hair, he just wanted to touch it and every woman wants to be touched." Another's husband was moved to take her out on the town to show her off after viewing the transformation that Rio engendered. Even Mary, the program's host, tells us that her hair was very "kinky, fuzzy and curly" and that as a result she was insecure and embarrassed to go on dates with her boyfriend. Clearly, the promise of Rio hair is closely aligned with the possibility of sexual desirability. That they wish to market a system of hair care and want customers to pay for their product only partially explains the undergirding ideologies exhibited here. In clear opposition to the group of African American women who advertised beauty during the beginning of this century, this product's manufacturer appears to believe that African Americans with hair in its natural state are in big trouble.

The hair in the "before" shots of the testimonials is telling: all of them show hair that is not styled, combed, conditioned, or cut. Frankly, it is hair like I have never before seen in my life, except in the previously discussed nineteenth-century mail-order beauty ads. The women and one man are pictured

Figs. 12 and 13. It's awesome.

without makeup, smiles, or attractive clothing. They look like wild, unhappy, unstylish, almost primitive people. It is a circumstance within which *any* change would be welcomed. The "after" shots feature women who have been given a complete beauty makeover, including designer clothes, makeup, cut, and style. Within this context, Rio hair takes on overtones associated with upward mobility, overall good grooming, and perhaps most significantly, the inherent benefits of a consumer lifestyle. Everyone shows that they are able to shake their hair, and they do so repeatedly with huge smiles plastered on their faces (figs. 14 and 15).

It is interesting that this infomercial was crafted during a period in which many noted the resurgence of the Afro. Newspapers nationwide reported a growing trend toward wearing an Afro and suggested that "the Afro—that bold and popular signature of political militancy and Black Power during the 1960s and '70s—is on the rebound." Although the general feeling surrounding these developments is that they have far more to do with fashion and much less to do with activism than earlier interests, many observers and Afro wearers say it represents a resurgence of black pride in our cultural heritage.[6] Rio's manufacturers do not appear to believe that Afro wearers are a consumer market worth targeting.

What is perhaps most disturbing about this infomercial is its striking similarity to early mail-order advertisements undergirded by blatantly racist assumptions. Today, however, the product's manufacturers have reworked this argument to position African American men as the prize at the end of the straightening rainbow. Even more disturbing is the fact that large numbers of African American women rushed to purchase such a product. What does it all mean? Certainly that there are many African American women who wish to have their hair move when they shake their head. Perhaps it also indicates that it is no longer necessary to address African American women in terms of kinship and overall enhancement to create a market for hair-care products. What this advertisement certainly indicates

Figs. 14 and 15. Shake your hair.

is that advertising discourses for African American hair-care products have, in some ways, come full circle.

It is possible to suggest that, during earlier periods, straightening of African American women's hair was an act of cultural syncretism, made up in equal parts by a desire to overcome the stigma of racially determined destiny and the desire for upward mobility. That is, at the dawn of the twentieth century, education and the means of producing work in the Western sense of the arts and sciences were largely unobtainable for the vast majority of African American women. An accessible way to meet this challenge to their humanity was through the only visible physical attribute that could be changed—their hair. Moreover, the scriptural mandate of hair as a woman's crown and glory further sanctioned such concerns. Even then, however, African American women found a way to market products that would fulfill such promises yet refrain from denigrating inherent characteristics of African American physiology and identity. Clearly, things have changed.

Although I am unsure what led to the widespread presence of African American women in the production, marketing, and selling of hair-care products at the turn of the century, it did not last long. By the 1940s, control of African American hair-care products returned by and large to those who, like the marketers of Rio, could find precious little to praise about our hair.

Hair Care Advertisements: 1940s and Beyond

Between 1940 and the present, African American hair-care products manufactured by African American–owned companies have outsold those of white-owned companies.[7] If the products produced similar results, this substantial in sales difference must speak, at some level, to the success of the African American companies' advertising strategies. From the late 1940s, with the rise of the liberal consensus in America and hegemonic integrationist legal and political efforts in African American culture, a notable ideological difference can be seen in

ads promoting products manufactured by white-owned as opposed to African American–owned companies. After a time,
however, both have the same battle cry: "Just straighten your
hair."

Although an economic analysis obviously lends itself to a
discussion of advertisements, the fact that there is a difference
between the profits of African American and white companies
in the area of hair-care products speaks to a difference in the
way African American women make meaning within that
capitalistic framework. Because there were few African American companies with the financial resources to advertise in national publications during the 1940s, I can include only two in
this discussion—Apex and Madam C. J. Walker. There were,
however, a number of white companies that advertised such
products.

For example, a 1948 Lustrasilk advertisement shows us that
the manufacturers wish African American women to believe
that their lives need to be and will be substantially changed by
the purchase of this product. If African American women want
a "different" life, complete with "beauty, comfort and lasting
peace of mind" as well as a "smile of confidence," they must use
this product. When we contrast this view with that of the
Madam C. J. Walker Company during the same year, we find a
great difference in the message. Walker's company says that her
products are "For Women of Beauty," whereas the white-owned
company emphasizes a "lack." African American women in
Walker's advertisement already possess beauty. This idea is
underscored by the model in Walker's advertisement. She is
pictured as a mature woman with short hair. It is a representation of African American female beauty that is more attainable
by a larger spectrum of the community.

In contrast, the model in the Lustrasilk ad looks like a young
debutante whose hairstyle emulates the ideals of the dominant
culture. Given this dichotomy, the fact that African American
women more frequently purchased products produced by African American companies speaks to an autonomous experience

and resistance to the meaning prescribed by the dominant culture. Taken alone, the slogan the Walker company used would seem to be a cliché without much significance. When we look at the ad as one in a series, a pattern begins to emerge.

Although Apex is an African American–owned company, its advertisement from 1948 portrays a model very similar to the one in the 1948 Lustrasilk advertisement. Indeed, the woman looks upper or upper-middle class, and her hairstyle is appropriate for either an African American or a white woman. However, the ad focuses on the Hairstyle of the Month—Mantilla. Most of the copy describes the romantic nature of Spain but also includes instructions on the way to achieve the style, the size roller needed, and so forth. No explicit claims are made about the changes that will happen after using this product. No mention is made of the hairstyle as somehow synonymous with beauty, confidence, or success. Indeed, only when we look at the small print in the corner do we find that to obtain this style, one must start with "smooth, lustrous, healthy hair."

This same strategy is repeated in a 1950 Apex advertisement. This time the model is a drawing and the copy appeals to "Those who care." The manufacturer tells us that this is the best product on the market, and they have done a survey to prove it. These two Apex ads can be contrasted with the 1955 Hair Strate ad, produced by a white-owned company. This ad for a chemical hair straightener promises "beauty for keeps" and says that "anyone can have a lovely hair style" with this product. Because the product uses chemicals to straighten hair permanently, a correlation is made between straight hair and beauty. To achieve this beauty and keep it, African American women are told they must change the texture of their hair drastically.

Surprisingly, or maybe not so, this same dichotomy exists in advertisements from the more militant, or revolutionary, 1970s. A Johnson Products Afro Sheen advertisement from 1971 exhibits similar advertising strategies. The slogan "Watu Wazuri use Afro Sheen" appears at the bottom of the page. In Swahili, this phrase means "Beautiful people use Afro Sheen." The advertisement begins with a Swahili saying, "Kama mama, kama binti," which means, "Like mother, like daughter." As a result, the "Afros" and "faces" of the mother and daughter signify beauty that spans generations back to Africa. A 1970 Clairol advertisement for the Afro promises to "free the 'fro," illustrating a clear co-optation of an African American vernacular expression as well as of political concerns.

While Afro Sheen appropriated Swahili to sell the product, it did so in the context of emphasizing an existent African American female beauty. The Clairol ad's use of African American vernacular not only trivializes the significance of African American political resistance but diminishes the political significance of the Afro itself. The Clairol Afro ad refigures the Lustrasilk strategy by repeating and revising what white-owned companies perceive as the problematic of African American hair. Lustrasilk promised beauty and success with soft, straight hair, and Clairol also emphasizes the need to have hair that is "high, wide and easy to comb." It points to the necessity of utilizing a product to make the "natural" bigger and better, that is, unnatural. Nowhere in this ad do we see an acknowledgment of African American female beauty; we see only that there is something "naturally" lacking that these products will fix.

Black Enterprise reports that between 1978 and 1988, the profit margin between white-owned and African American–owned companies narrowed.[8] One possible indicator of the seriousness of the white companies' threat to the "clout" that African American companies once enjoyed may be the fact that over twenty African American hair-care and cosmetic manufacturers organized themselves into the American Health and Beauty Aids Institute. During this same ten-year period, the construction of African American female beauty became very similar in both white and African American companies' advertisements for hair-care products. No longer were allowances made for an existent beauty, and after the early 1980s, there were no more calls for leaving one's hair in its natural condition. African American women's hair must be straightened.

In a 1988 Lustrasilk ad for the Nature Wave product, the model tells us that "Mother Nature didn't give me this style, Nature Wave did." She then goes on to boast that the product makes it difficult for someone to tell if her hair is naturally straight or has been chemically treated. No longer is it enough to have straight hair; but now it must somehow be able to fool others into believing it is natural. Likewise, a 1988 Alberto Culver ad tells us we need hair that is not only straight but "bone strait." One obvious result of such advertising discourses is the previously mentioned infomerical for Rio hair-care products. There are, however, others.

For example, an African American writer for the *New York Times* recently described an incident that took place while she was baby-sitting her five-year-old niece. After playing hairdresser with two dolls, one white and one black, this writer was disturbed to discover that her niece preferred the hair texture of the white doll to that of the black. Although sad, this turn of events is far from shocking. It is a circumstance that seems to have remained relatively constant for hundreds of years. Moreover, the writer was even familiar with the various doll studies and knew she should not have been surprised. She was also familiar with the explanations for such preferences and went on to say that they stem "in part, from the days of the 'privileged' slaves, who inherited light skin and straight hair, as well as land and a misplaced sense of self-worth, from their masters."[9]

None of this is new. What is noteworthy, however, is that the writer, while at the beauty parlor waiting to get a relaxer, rethought her niece's response to African American hair. Although she was saddened to think about the message her own straight hair sent her niece, she did not get up and leave. Neither knowledge of the past nor concern about the future was enough to convince her not to straighten her hair. Perhaps with time, such an incident will appear minor. Perhaps in a distant future, a newly minted Ph.D., working on her first book, will place this anecdote in historical context and show that there is more here than meets the eye. Perhaps I am just too close to feel anything but sadness for a five-year-old girl who already believes her body is imperfect and has that belief reinforced by a successful African American role model who is unable to imagine the possibility of not straightening her hair.

In another incident, a young reporter writes about her fascination with long hair and the role of the media in fostering that desire. While still a young child, she noticed that black fashion models were generally photographed wearing long, straight wigs. She adds that, "without knowing it, the media had conditioned my young mind to think that you're only beautiful if you have long hair. I reasoned that if I wanted to be considered pretty, I had to grow some hair." She goes on to report that since the media has begun to spotlight actress Halle Berry and singer Toni Braxton, both beautiful, young black women who sport smart, short styles that highlight black facial features, she has decided to wear her hair short. This "doesn't make me feel like a conformist, but rather an attractive young woman. That's a real breakthrough for me."[10] This young woman's selective dependence on media images is interesting in that it does not appear to include celebrities who do not wear their hair straightened. Have we reached a point where the only acceptable option for African American women is straight hair? Is this the legacy of Madam C. J. Walker and her ilk?

If competing understandings of acceptable expressions of female identity are in some respects central in coming to understand the significance of hair in contemporary times, generational differences are also a factor. Publications such as *Vibe* magazine, marketed to the hip-hop generation, are a telling source of hair politics. Its primary focus is music, with a heavy emphasis on rap artists and young entertainers who subscribe to the style of music considered "New Jack."

In the second anniversary issue of *Vibe*, an article reports that the hip-hop generation is much more likely to champion hair that has not been straightened. The article features a number of performers who explain that their stance on hair straightening is widely shared by their contemporaries and very much influenced by their reading and understanding of history as well as by their desire to be more Afrocentric. The article adds that "hip hop has taken hair back to its African roots. From dreads, cornrows, and braids to twists, coils to 'fros, hip hop is keeping it real . . . natural. For many, hair is more than just a style—it's a statement."[11]

Later in that same issue, however, is a photo layout titled "Non-Blonds," picturing a number of African American singers who not only straighten their hair but dye it blond. In the first article, all but one of the performers who declare their generation to be chemical free are men; the "non-blonds" are primarily women. The question then becomes whether this contradiction merely exemplifies a blending of postmodern ideas about identity construction and Afrocentricity available to this hip-hop generation or whether it speaks to a gender split within that generation. In any case, if more contemporary advertisers for beauty products and African American purchasers of such products have assigned meanings to hair that speak to gender and generation, then the meaning of hair has changed over time. It is clear, however, that hair raises a myriad of concerns and speaks volumes about various tensions and issues in African American communities. This has long been the case.

Since at least the turn of the century, African American women have utilized visual representations of themselves and other African American women to construct racial and gender identities that broaden our understanding of the distinguishing characteristics of black womanhood. At the turn of the century, racial ideologies posited specific relationships between skin color, hair texture, and the possibilities for intelligence, social advancement, and cultural acceptance. As a result, advertisements for products aimed at changing skin color or hair texture asked African Americans to disavow attributes that would identify them as having an African ancestry. These advertisements most often relied on images of African American women to illustrate the necessity of such a move.

During this same period, male intellectuals and leaders within African American middle-class communities challenged the primacy of racial ideologies that linked the possibility of social mobility to physiology. In turn, they urged middle-class African Americans to heighten their efforts at cultural production to mediate damaging representations within the dominant society. They too used African American women's bodies as examples of why such production was urgently needed, pointing out the psychological damage inflicted on those who attempt to follow societal prescriptions for beauty.

On the one hand, beauty product manufacturers utilized African American female bodies to articulate the need for and societal rewards of products aimed at lessening the shame of African American ancestry. On the other hand, in critiquing such ideologies, male members of African American communities appropriated those same bodies to exemplify the urgent need of increased cultural production on the part of the African American middle class. In both cases, during the Progressive Era, African American female bodies become an entity, pressed into the service of differing ideologies and political agendas. Within this debate, it becomes difficult to fathom the meaning, for individual African American women, of the bodies, and the articulation of an African American female identity is muted.

By 1905, African American women began to advertise beauty products for women whose race and gender they shared. Their advertising campaigns relied almost exclusively on photographic images of themselves, and their practices of identity construction and representation reshaped the terrain upon which the cultural significance of their bodies had been built. Indeed, these self-representations functioned to critique racial ideologies that identified African American female bodies as a "lack" or that disavowed African ancestry. Their presence in African American newspapers was an example of the type of cultural production that male middle-class ideologues championed.

However, because these women were often working or lower class, their advertisements functioned to wrest control of a definition of oppositional cultural production from middle-class male ideals and to reposition such production in relationship to a working-class female discourse. As a result, the pages of African American periodicals became a discursive site within which African American female identity was consistently (re)articulated, and by far the primary attribute around which these discourses swirled was hair.

Most often the photographs that accompanied hair advertisements produced by African American women pictured dark-skinned, big-boned African American women who were discussed and presented as the standard of beauty for which readers should strive. As well, they infused their ads with culturally specific symbology that would have been readily identifiable to an African American readership.

What becomes significant here are the ways that African American women used hair advertisements as an occasion to construct an identity and communicate meaning about the significance of their bodies in African American communities. Indeed, as we look closely at the advertising campaigns of Madam C. J. Walker, certainly one of most successful advertisers of the day, it is apparent that, along with concerns about beauty standards, she is anxious that African American women gain a level of economic independence. For Walker, independence came to denote not only freedom from economic dependance on dominant culture but also freedom from individual African American men within the institution of marriage.

By urging African American women to join her in the business sphere, she threatened hegemonic ideals surrounding the meaning of domesticity and acceptable behavior for those women. As a result, gender was highlighted, and Walker was able to propose alternative prescriptions for an acceptable African American female identity. By focusing on attributes other than those generally connected with "New Negros" or the elite professional class of African Americans committed to defining identities for an African American populace, Walker broadened "acceptable" public representations and identities of African American women.

Walker was concerned with the place of African American women within both the public and the private spheres, and the editors and writers of *Woman's Voice* functioned as a mouthpiece for her views, without the restraint of a star image. They offered specific strategies African American women might find useful in their lives, and they constructed identities that functioned to address and at times challenge hegemonic ideals surrounding African American female identity within African American communities.

Hair then, or the culturally specific articulations and uses of hair as a symbol of African American female identity, has a long history. Indeed, advertising hair products offered African American women the opportunity to shape identities, broaden representations of those identities, and communicate culturally specific meanings of the significance of those identities, and, by extension, African American women's place within American as well as African American culture. Thus, hair offers an opportunity to examine the politics of African American women's bodies and the representation of those bodies, and we are better able to fathom what they meant to African American women. So, if a contemporary African American female movie reviewer wishes to reduce the significance of a film that raises and (re)articulates revolutionary iconographies of African American female identity and beauty to hair, she may be closer to the truth than she understands. Hair raises just these types of concerns.

Afterword

*I*n October 1988, while attending church, my grandmother suffered a major stroke. The person who called suggested that I take the next available flight out of Iowa City as "things don't look good." In between trying to maintain some level of composure and frantically pushing back the possibility that she would not survive, and possibly even die before I could get to Florida, I diverted my attention by putting together a rationale I could offer her as to why I had decided to let my hair "lock." Surprisingly (or maybe not), this topic managed to keep me occupied and relatively hysteria free during the hours of travel.

When I arrived at the hospital, I was met by my father, who stopped me outside her door to let me know her condition. She was alive but unable to speak. He also told me that she was confused and unable to recognize those around her, and they weren't sure how much she understood when spoken to. I pushed open the door, plastered one of those terrified smiles on my face, and prepared for the worst. I walked over to the bed and touched her shoulder. My grandmother turned in my direction, opened her eyes, and said quite clearly, "Oh my lord, what did you do to your hair?"

My grandmother died late in 1993. I remember this incident now as I look at a small ball of her hair I pulled from a brush following her death—a small gray and black puff that rests near a photograph of her. Soon after returning from her funeral, I cut a few inches off of my own, now shoulder-length, dreadlocks. They rest beside her picture and her hair. Now, as I end a long process she encouraged me to begin almost eight years ago but did not live to see me complete, I offer the above remembrance as an explanation of the meaning of hair in my own life. Grandma, it is done.

Notes

1   NAPPI BY NATURE

1. Gloria Wade-Gayles, "The Making of a Permanent Afro," *Catalyst: A Magazine of Heart and Mind* (Summer 1988): 20.

2. Alice Walker, "Oppressed Hair Puts a Ceiling on the Brain," in Alice Walker, *Living by the Word* (New York: Harcourt Brace Jovanovich, 1988), 70.

3. Mary Helen Washington, ed., *Invented Lives: Narratives of Black Women, 1860–1960* (Garden City, N.Y.: Doubleday, 1987), 249.

4. Willi M. Coleman, "Among the Things That Use to Be," in *Home Girls: A Black Feminist Anthology,* ed. Barbara Smith (New York: Kitchen Table: Women of Color Press, 1983), 221–222.

5. bell hooks, "Straightening Our Hair," *Z Magazine* (Summer 1988): 14.

6. Andrea Benton Rushing, "Hair-Raising," *Feminist Studies* 14 (Summer 1988): 325–335.

7. Roland Marchand, *Advertising the American Dream: Making Way for Modernity, 1920–1940* (Berkeley: University of California Press, 1985), xix.

8. Barbara Welch-Breeder, "Being-in-the-Body: A Reflection upon American Self-Medication in Drug Advertising," Ph.D. dissertation, University of Iowa, 1984, p. 7.

9. Magazines and newspapers produced by African Americans "have been vehicles for protest and creative expression while also being heavily influenced by the changing status and condition of Blacks in American society." Several scholars have documented how this has functioned historically. Dwight Brooks's history of African American magazines emphasizes the ways in which the magazines were influenced by the layout and content of white publications. He also points out the differences in financial backing: white magazines depended on economic support from corporate advertisers, whereas

black magazines and newspapers relied on economic support from such institutions as the church and schools or colleges. In addition, the African American press depended heavily on subscriptions, local advertising from small businesses, and the solicitation of shares in stock companies. Periodicals that did not have such crucial types of support often folded at the rate of one a year. Dwight Brooks, "Consumer Markets and Consumer Magazines," Ph.D. dissertation, University of Iowa, 1991, pp. 79–81. See also Abby Johnson and Ronald Johnson, *Propaganda and Aesthetics: The Literary Politics of Afro-American Magazines in the Twentieth Century* (Boston: University of Massachusetts Press, 1979).

10. This subject is dealt with extensively in Elizabeth V. Spelman, *The Inessential Woman: Problems of Exclusion in Feminist Thought* (Boston: Beacon Press, 1988).

11. Susan Brownmiller, "Hair," in *Femininity* (New York: Simon and Schuster, 1984), 32–61.

12. "Can Science Tell Negro Blood? Dr. Boas Has Hard Task," *New York Age* (December 31, 1914): 1. I searched through the first few months of 1915 issues to see if there was any mention of this topic being resolved, but there appear to have been no follow-up articles.

13. Cornel West, "The New Cultural Politics of Difference," in *Out There: Marginalization and Contemporary Cultures* (New York: New Museum of Contemporary Art, 1990), 28.

14. Stuart Hall, "Cultural Identity and Cinematic Representation," *Framework* 36 (Winter 1986): 69.

15. See Fox-Genovese's *Within the Plantation Household,* White's *Aren't I a Woman,* Bynum's *Unruly Women,* and Giddings's *When and Where I Enter* to name but a few of the works that advance our understanding of lives and relationships during the antebellum period.

2 BEAUTY, RACE, AND BLACK PRIDE

1. Charlotte F. Grimké, *The Journals of Charlotte Forten Grimké,* ed. Brenda Stevenson (New York: Oxford University Press, 1988), 33, 36.

2. Elizabeth Fox-Genovese, *Within the Plantation Household: Black and White Women of the Old South* (Chapel Hill: University of North Carolina Press, 1988), 216.

3. The advertisements discussed in this section are taken from the *St. Louis Palladium.* The *Palladium* was an African American newspaper that operated from 1896 through 1922. Although many of these advertisements can be found in newspapers from Maryland, Georgia, California, Colorado, and other states, I have chosen this particular newspaper because two of the women I discuss later, Madam C. J. Walker and Madam Annie T. Malone, lived in St. Louis between 1900 and 1906. These advertisements are probably ones to which they

would have had access during those periods. Both of these women advertised their own hair-care products widely and (re)produced competing constructions of African American women, so the advertisements and marketing strategies they probably saw in this newspaper, and which they ultimately critique, constitute a reasonable starting point.

4. The *Anglo-African Magazine* was published between 1859 and 1862. The publication featured scholarly articles, short fiction, and poems by such authors as Martin Delany, Frederick Douglass, John Langston, Frances Harper, and William Wells Brown. The magazine's goal was to find "men and women whose hearts are the homes of a high and lofty enthusiasm, and noble devotion to the cause of emancipation, who are ready and willing to lay time, talent and money on the altar of universal freedom." Wilson was writing for a population of free African Americans in the North (the magazine was published in Rochester, New York), and this article was probably read by whites and African Americans who were committed financially and emotionally to abolition.

5. Quoted in Waldo E. Martin, Jr., *The Mind of Frederick Douglass* (Chapel Hill: University of North Carolina Press, 1984), 239.

6. Quoted in Michael Banton, *Racial Theories* (New York: Cambridge University Press, 1987), 52.

7. George Stocking, Jr., *Race, Culture and Evolution* (New York: Free Press, 1968), 122.

8. Quoted in Dorothy Sterling, *We Are Your Sisters: Black Women in the Nineteenth Century* (New York: Norton, 1984), 429.

9. Evelyn Brooks-Higginbotham, *Righteous Discontent: The Woman's Movement in the Black Baptist Church, 1880–1920* (Cambridge: Harvard University Press, 1993), 216.

10. Jacqueline Bobo, *Black Women as Cultural Readers* (New York: Columbia University Press, 1995), 12.

3 ADVERTISING CONTRADICTIONS

1. Bills, Receipts, and Financial Ledgers, Madam C. J. Walker Collection, Indiana Historical Society, Indianapolis, Indiana. Hereafter referred to as the Walker Collection.

2. A'Lelia Bundles, *Madam C. J. Walker: Entrepreneur* (New York: Chelsea House Publishers, 1991).

3. Madam C. J. Walker, "Hints To Agents," Walker Collection.

4. Much of the information regarding Walker's attendance at this convention comes from articles that Walker's great-great-granddaughter, A'Lelia Perry Bundles, has written as well as from a biography she has authored for young adults. See Bundles, *Madam C. J. Walker*, 11–15;

and idem, "Madam C. J. Walker—Cosmetics Tycoon," *Ms. Magazine* (July 1983): 91. To date hers is the most comprehensive work on Walker's life.

5. Quoted in August Meier, *Negro Thought in America, 1880–1915: Racial Ideologies in the Age of Booker T. Washington* (Ann Arbor: University of Michigan Press, 1966), 9.

Du Bois proclaimed his allegiance to socialism in 1904. However, according to Manning Marable, he believed that the African American entrepreneurial elite was basically a powerful means of battling discrimination. Indeed, in a conference of business leaders held in Philadelphia in 1913, he concluded that despite evidence of "a spirit of aggrandizement, lying, stealing and grafting," the general outlook for this stratum was "excellent." In 1922 and 1928, he published articles in *Crisis* which applauded the development of black-owned and -directed banks. It was only after the Great Depression that Du Bois grew pessimistic about the long-term possibility of a "Black Capitalist Solution" to the Negro's plight. See Manning Marable, *How Capitalism Underdeveloped Black America* (Boston: South End Press, 1983), 133–167, for a fuller discussion of Du Bois's relationship to capitalism as a strategy for racial uplift.

6. Washington had achieved a national reputation even before his famous 1895 address at the Atlanta Cotton Exposition. In this address, he asserted that African Americans should work within the South's system of segregation and not be concerned with agitating for social rights. After this speech, he became a "spokesman" on race. He accomplished this in part by gaining control of a number of African American newspapers and periodicals and using them to spread his message of accommodation. Among the periodicals he used to propagandize his approach to race relations was the *New York Age*.

7. Quoted in *The Booker T. Washington Papers*, vol. 11, *1911–1912*, ed. Louis R. Harlan and Raymond Smock (Urbana: University of Illinois Press, 1981), 420.

8. Madam C. J. Walker was one of the first cosmetic manufacturers and women whom Washington allowed to participate in his organization. She was also the first woman to hold a position on the board of trustees of Tuskeegee Institute, but she was not appointed until a few months after Washington's death.

9. Bundles, *Madam C. J. Walker*, 67.

10. *The Madam C. J. Walker Beauty Manual: A Thorough Treatise Covering All Branches of Beauty Culture*, Schomburg Center for Research in Black Culture, New York Public Library, Microfilm R-2412, p. 24.

11. Quoted in Beverly Guy-Sheftall, *Daughters of Sorrow: Attitudes toward Black Women, 1880–1920* (New York: Carlson Publishing, 1990), 96.

12. Quoted in Lawson Scruggs, *Women of Distinction* (Raleigh, N.C.: L. A. Scruggs, 1893), xi.

13. Fred Moore, "How to Keep Women at Home," *Colored American Magazine* 14 (January 1908): 7–8.

14. Thomas Nelson Baker, "The Negro Woman," *Alexander's Magazine* 2 (December 15, 1906): 84.

15. Her desire to socialize the company appear to have been relatively short-lived. Although she invited delegates to her first annual convention in 1917, saying that plans to turn the company into a cooperative would be discussed and outlined, this discussion does not appear on the program and there is no further mention of this endeavor. I am not suggesting that Walker was ever a socialist. See Instructions to Agents Before 1919, Walker Collection.

16. Formation of National Negro Cosmetic Manufacturers Association, dated September 5, 1917, Walker Collection.

17. Louis B. George, "Beauty Culture and Colored People," *Messenger* (July 1918): 18.

4 BROADENING REPRESENTATIONAL BOUNDARIES

1. Marcus Garvey, "The Colored or Negro Press," in *Philosophy and Opinions of Marcus Garvey*, vol. 2, ed. Amy Jacque-Garvey (New York: Atheneum Press, 1971), 79.

2. "Queen of Gotham's Colored 400," *Literary Digest* 55 (October 13, 1917): 75–78. The title of this article refers to the four hundred wealthiest African Americans in New York.

3. Kevin Gains, "Assimilationist Minstrelsy as Racial Uplift Ideology," *American Quarterly* 45 (September 1993): 22–35.

4. Quoted in Beverly Guy-Sheftall, *Daughters of Sorrow: Attitudes toward Black Women, 1880–1920* (New York: Carlson Publishing, 1990), 142.

5. Evelyn Brooks-Higginbotham, in a chapter titled "The Female Talented Tenth," argues that this preoccupation with education cut across class lines and varying ideological positions related to the advancement of "the Race." She suggests that this was true because education was perceived as offering the possibility for collective empowerment, and therefore, "Education, especially higher education, was considered essential to the progress of African Americans as a group." What is significant for Brooks-Higginbotham, however, are the ways in which education and the discussion of its necessity had the effect of promoting middle-class values and Victorian sensibilities among newly freed African Americans. See Evelyn Brooks-Higginbotham, *Righteous Discontent: The Women's Movement in the Black Baptist Church, 1880–1920* (Cambridge: Harvard University Press, 1993), 19–46.

6. See letters dated 15 September 1918, Walker Collection. These letters were exchanged by the editors of the *Washington Bee,* the *Colorado Statesman,* and F. B. Ransom. See also the letter from Madam C. J. Walker dated October 1918 in which she asks Ransom to remind both editors of the amount of advertising dollars she spent with their papers.

7. "Mme. Walker Returns From New England Tour," *New York Age* (November 12, 1914): 1. See also undated press release, Walker Collection, which is substantially similar to the above article.

8. "Wealthiest Negro Woman's Suburban Mansion," *Messenger* (June 1918): 2. The same article, now titled "Mme. Walker's Purchase of New Estate," appears in the *New York Age* (September 6, 1918): 1.

9. Madam C. J. Walker, letter to F. B. Ransom, 9 March 1918, Walker Collection.

10. Madame C. J. Walker, undated press release, Walker Collection.

11. Richard Dyer, *Heavenly Bodies: Film Stars and Society* (New York: St. Martin's Press, 1986), 2–3. However, unlike most stars, Walker maintained a high level of activity in her star-image construction. As a result, she was able to use that image in ways she believed most beneficial.

12. Madam C. J. Walker, letter to F. B. Ransom, September 1918, Walker Collection.

13. Madam C. J. Walker, letter to F. B. Ransom, 2 November 1916, Walker Collection.

14. Madam C. J. Walker, letter to F. B. Ransom, 12 April 1918, Walker Collection.

15. Madam C. J. Walker, letter to F. B. Ransom, 29 October 1915, Walker Collection.

16. Madam C. J. Walker, Special Agents Contract, Walker Collection.

17. Madam C. J. Walker, letter to F. B. Ransom, 9 September 1915, Walker Collection.

18. Alice Burnett, letters to Walker Manufacturing Company, 7 August 1917 and 6 September 1917, Walker Collection.

19. Brooks-Higginbotham, *Righteous Discontent,* 6–7.

20. Madam C. J. Walker, letters to F. B. Ransom, July 1915 and 29 October 1915, Walker Collection.

21. Expense sheets for 1912–1914, 1918, and 1919, Walker Collection. See also Reports of Receipt and Expenses, and Adjustments and Closings, Walker Collection.

22. Madam C. J. Walker, letter to F. B. Ransom, 15 December 1916, Walker Collection.

23. Madam C. J. Walker, letter to F. B. Ransom, 1 December 1916, Walker Collection. Alice Kelly was a supervisor and responsible for

mixing and boxing the various preparations. Turner worked the delivery truck and mailed the preparations.

24. A'Lelia Bundles, *Madam C. J. Walker: Entrepreneur* (New York: Chelsea House Publishers, 1991), 56.

25. Madam C. J. Walker, letter to F. B. Ransom, 15 December 1916, Walker Collection. For examples of letters regarding the responses and questions of college presidents, see letters addressed to Walker Manufacturing Company, dated 15, 22, and 29 March, 5 April, and 25 August 1917, Walker Collection.

26. Bundles, *Madam C. J. Walker,* 40.

27. Last Will and Testament of Madam C. J. Walker, Walker Collection.

28. A'Lelia Walker Robinson, Madam's only daughter, left similar instructions in her will. She also argued with the company attorney, F. B. Ransom, over a substantial sum of money she wanted to leave to Ransom's daughter and refused to allow him or the child's older brothers to control the trust fund. The matter was resolved by appointing Ransom's wife as trustee for the funds. Ransom's boys were left nothing. A'Lelia justified her position by stating that boys are not as reliable or as trustworthy as women. These are but a few examples of the ways these women structured a woman-centered identity.

5   GENDER, HAIR, AND AFRICAN AMERICAN WOMEN'S MAGAZINES

1. Margaret Thompson, letter to F. B. Ransom, 9 August 1917, Walker Collection. Walker, and by extension her company, made a commitment to support the magazine until such time as it could support itself.

2. Kathryn Shevelow, *Women and Print Culture: The Construction of Femininity in the Early Periodical* (New York: Routledge, 1989), 4.

3. Dwight Brooks, "Consumer Markets and Consumer Magazines: Black America and the Culture of Consumption, 1920–1960," Ph.D. dissertation, University of Iowa, 1991, p. 27. See also E. Franklin Frazier, *Black Bourgeoisie* (New York: Krause-Thomson Organization Ltd., 1973), 34; and Abby Johnson and Ronald Johnson, *Propaganda and Aesthetics: The Literary Politics of Afro American Magazines in the Twentieth Century* (Boston: University of Massachusetts Press, 1979), 52, for a full discussion of the ways African American periodicals functioned to prescribe behavior for new immigrants.

4. Nicholas Lemann, *The Promised Land: The Great Black Migration and How It Changed America* (New York: Vintage Books, 1992), 16.

5. Hazel Carby, "Policing the Black Woman's Body in an Urban Context," *Critical Inquiry* (Summer 1992): 739–755.

6. For example, in the 1910 census, 60 percent of African American women responding reported that they either were married or had been

at one time. Among women between the ages of thirty-four and thirty-seven, the number rose to 91.8 percent. In 1920, the number of married women dropped slightly to 58.5 percent, with 15.9 percent listing their status as widowed and 2.2 percent saying they were divorced. During these same periods, roughly 61 percent of the women responding listed their occupation as something other than work outside the home.

7. During this period, there were other magazines aimed at an African American female reading public. *Our Women and Children* was established in 1888 and was followed in 1891 by *Ringwood's Afro-American Journal of Fashion*. During the first decade of the twentieth century, two more periodicals made their debut. In 1900, *Woman's World* was issued, and in 1907 the *Colored Woman's Magazine* was founded. All four are said to have been monthly family magazines. Of these four publications, copies exist for *Our Women and Children,* but none have been located for the others. Of these women's magazines, *Half-Century* was perhaps the most well known.

8. Johnson and Johnson, *Propaganda and Aesthetics,* 48.

9. *Half-Century Magazine* (August 1916): 1.

10. This editorial focus on business may have had something to do with the financial backing the magazine received from Anthony Overton, an African American cosmetics manufacturer and bank owner in the Chicago area. Indeed, almost half of the products advertised in *Half-Century* were manufactured by Overton's firm. As well, there are advertisements for Overton's Victory Life Insurance Company and Douglass National Bank. His salesmen and agents and their accomplishments were also highlighted frequently. Although it appears that Overton's relationship with the magazine was purely financial, he and his companies received quite a lot of coverage and, by extension, free advertising.

11. "The Care of the Hair," *Half-Century Magazine* (September 1916): 11.

12. Madam C. J. Walker, letter to F. B. Ransom, 10 April 1916, Walker Collection.

13. Madam C. J. Walker, letter to F. B. Ransom, 18 June 1916, Walker Collection.

14. Walker Manufacturing Company, External Correspondence, October 1920, Walker Collection.

15. Walker Company Adjustments and Closing entries, 31 December 1920, Walker Collection. It is interesting that *Woman's Voice* figures were listed here along with advertising figures for the Walker Company. Looking at copies of the magazine, it becomes clear that there was more than a casual relationship between the publication and the Walker Company. For example, although the magazine was published in Philadelphia, the Advertising Solicitor/Business Manager's address

is listed as 640 North West Street in Indianapolis, the address of the Walker Manufacturing Company's main headquarters. This is also the address listed for the circulation department of *Woman's Voice*.

16. *Woman's Voice* (January 1921): 12.

17. Ellen McCracken, "The Cover: Window to the Future Self," in *Decoding Women's Magazines: From Mademoiselle to Ms.* (New York: St. Martin's Press, 1993), 13–14.

18. *Woman's Voice* (December 1919): 12.

19. "Who Can Guess a Man," *Woman's Voice* (March 1922): 20.

20. *Woman's Voice* (December 1921): 5.

21. "The Only Way to Hold a Man," *Woman's Voice* (December 1921): 14.

22. "Back Numbers," *Woman's Voice* (March 1922): 16.

23. *Woman's Voice* (March 1922): 7.

24. Ros Ballaster, Margaret Beetham, Elizabeth Frazer, and Sandra Hebron, *Women's Worlds: Ideology, Femininity and the Woman's Magazine* (London: Macmillan, 1991), 1.

6 IN SEARCH OF CONNECTIONS

1. Quoted in Greg Tate, "Of Homegirl Goddesses and Geechee Women," *Village Voice*, June 4, 1991, pp. 72, 78.

2. "Black Women Outspend on Hair," *Minority Markets Alert* (September 1994): 1.

3. *New York Times*, June 8, 1995, p. 5.

4. *The Baltimore Sun*, November 10, 1994, p. 25A.

5. "Scalp Woes Unite Women Suing Rio Hair-Care Company," *Dayton Daily News*, April 25, 1995, p. 10C.

6. *Chicago Sun-Times*, July 21, 1994.

7. Grayson Mitchell, "Battle of the Rouge," *Black Enterprise* (August 1978): 23–29.

8. "Black Enterprise Top 100 Black Businesses," *Black Enterprise* (June 1988): 106–109.

9. Robin D. Stone, "Washing a Doll's Head and Untangling a Dream," *New York Times*, June 8, 1995, p. 6.

10. Kia Stokes, "Bad Hair Days Gone at Last," *Baltimore Sun*, November 10, 1994, p. 24A.

11. Delphine Fawundu, "Hair: Hip Hop Hairdos," *Vibe* (August 1995): 158.

Selected Bibliography

BOOKS AND JOURNAL ARTICLES

Adams, John H., Jr. "A Study of the Features of the New Negro Woman." *Voice of the Negro* 8 (August 1904): 323–327.

Alcoff, Linda. "Cultural Feminism Versus Poststructuralism: The Identity Crisis in Feminist Theory." *Signs* 13 (Fall 1988): 405–436.

Alexander, Priscilla, and Frederique Delacoste, eds. *Sex Work: Writings By Women in the Sex Industry.* Pittsburgh, Pa.: Cleis Press, 1987.

Althusser, Louis. "Ideology and Ideological State Apparatuses." *Lenin and Philosophy,* 127–186. New York and London: Monthly Review Press, 1970.

Baker, Thomas Nelson. "The Negro Woman." *Alexander's Magazine* 2 (December 15, 1906): 84–85.

Ballister, Ros, Margaret Beetham, Elizabeth Frazer, and Sandra Hebron. *Women's Worlds: Ideology, Femininity and the Woman's Magazine.* London: Macmillan, 1991.

Banner, Lois, *American Beauty.* Chicago: University of Chicago Press, 1983.

Banton, Michael. *Racial Theories.* New York and London: Cambridge University Press, 1987.

Barthel, Diane. *Putting on Appearances: Gender and Advertising.* Philadelphia: Temple University Press, 1988.

Berkhofer, Robert F. "A New Context for a New American Studies." *American Quarterly* 41 (Fall 1989): 558–613.

Bobo, Jacqueline. "Reading through the Text: The Black Woman as Audience." In *Black American Cinema,* ed. Manthia Diawara, 272–287. New York: Routledge, 1993.

Bordo, Susan. "Material Girl: The Effacements of Postmodern Culture." In Susan Bordo, *Unbearable Weight: Feminism, Western Culture, and the Body,* 245–275. Berkeley: University of California Press, 1993.

150   *Selected Bibliography*

————. "Reading the Slender Body." *Body Politics: Women and the Discourses of Science,* ed. Mary Jacobus, Evelyn Fox Keller, and Sally Shuttleworth, 83–112. New York: Routledge, 1990.

Braithwaite, Deborah, and Roger Willis. *VanDerZee: Photographer, 1886–1983.* New York: Harry N. Abrams, 1993.

Brooks, Dwight. "Consumer Markets and Consumer Magazines: Black America and the Culture of Consumption, 1920–1960." Ph.D. dissertation, University of Iowa, 1991.

Brooks-Higginbotham, Evelyn. "African American Women's History and the Metalanguage of Race." *Signs* 17 (Winter 1992): 251–274.

————. *Righteous Discontent: The Woman's Movement in the Black Baptist Church, 1880–1920.* Cambridge: Harvard University Press, 1993.

Brownmiller, Susan, "Hair." In *Femininity,* 32–61. New York: Simon and Schuster, 1984.

Bundles, A'Lelia Perry. "Madam C. J. Walker—Cosmetics Tycoon." *Ms. Magazine* (July 1983): 91.

————. *Madam C. J. Walker, Entrepreneur.* New York: Chelsea House Publishers, 1991.

Bynum, Victoria E. *Unruly Women: The Politics of Social & Sexual Control in the Old South.* Chapel Hill: University of North Carolina Press, 1992.

Carbine, Mary. " 'The Finest Outside the Loop': Motion Picture Exhibition in Chicago's Black Metropolis, 1905–1928." *Camera Obscura* 23 (1990): 9–41.

Carby, Hazel. "Policing the Black Woman's Body in an Urban Context." *Critical Inquiry* 18 (Summer 1992): 739–755.

————. *Reconstructing Womanhood: The Emergence of the Afro-American Woman Novelist.* New York: Oxford University Press, 1987.

Chapkis, Wendy. *Beauty Secrets.* Boston: South End Press, 1986.

Christian, Barbara. *Black Feminist Criticism: Perspectives on Black Women Writers.* New York: Pergamon Press, 1985.

————. *Black Women Novelists: The Development of a Tradition, 1892–1976.* Westport, Conn.: Greenwood Press, 1980.

————. "The Race for Theory." *Feminist Studies* 14, 1 (1988): 67–69.

Collins, Patricia Hill. *Black Feminist Thought: Knowledge, Consciousness, and the Politics of Empowerment.* New York: Routledge, 1990.

Cooper, Wendy. *Hair: Sex, Society, Symbolism.* New York: Stein and Day, 1971.

Craig, Leo. "The Changing Communicative Structure of Advertisements, 1850–1930." Ph.D. dissertation, University of Iowa, 1985.

Cruz, Jon. "Testimonies and Artifacts: Elite Appropriations of African American Music in the Nineteenth Century." In *Viewing, Reading, Listening: Audiences and Cultural Reception,* ed. Jon Cruz and Justin Lewis, 125–150. San Francisco: Westview Press, 1994.

de Lauretis, Teresa. *Techologies of Gender: Essays on Theory, Film, and Fiction*. Bloomington: University of Indiana Press, 1987.

Diawara, Manthia. "Black Spectatorship: Problems of Identification and Resistance." In *Black American Cinema*, ed. Manthia Diawara, 211–220. New York: Routledge, 1993.

Du Bois, W.E.B. *The Souls of Black Folks*. New York: Krause-Thomson Organization Ltd., 1973.

Dyer, Richard. *Heavenly Bodies: Film Stars and Society*. New York: St. Martin's Press, 1986.

Dyson, Michael Eric. *Reflecting Black: African American Cultural Criticism*. Minneapolis: University of Minnesota Press, 1993.

Epstein, Barbara. "Family, Sexual Morality, and Popular Movements in Turn-of-the Century America." In *Powers of Desire: The Politics of Sexuality*, ed. Ann Snitow, Christine Stansell, and Sharon Thompson, 117–130. New York: Monthly Review Press, 1983.

Ewen, Stuart. *Captains of Consciousness: Advertising and the Social Roots of the Consumer Culture*. New York: McGraw-Hill, 1976.

Ferguson, Margorie. *Forever Feminine: Women's Magazines and the Cult of Femininity*. London: Heinemann, 1983.

Fox-Genovese, Elizabeth. *Within the Plantation Household: Black and White Women of the Old South*. Chapel Hill: University of North Carolina Press, 1988.

Frazier, Franklin E. *Black Bourgeoisie*. New York: Krause-Thomson Organization Ltd., 1973.

Freeman, Martin. "Beauty." *Anglo-African Magazine* (April 12, 1859): 7–8.

Gains, Jane. "Fire and Desire: Race, Melodrama, and Oscar Micheaux." In *Black American Cinema*, ed. Manthia Diawara, 49–70. New York: Routledge, 1993.

Gains, Kevin. "Assimilationist Minstrelsy as Racial Uplift Ideology." *American Quarterly* 45 (September 1993): 22–35.

Gates, Henry Louis. "The Trope of the New Negro and the Reconstruction of the Image of the Black." *Representations* 12 (Fall 1988): 122–157.

———. "The Master's Pieces: On Canon Formation and the African American Tradition." In *Loose Cannons: Notes on the Culture Wars*, 17–42. New York: Oxford University Press, 1992.

Geertz, Clifford. *The Interpretation of Cultures*. New York: Basic Books, 1973.

George, Louis W. "Beauty Culture and Colored People." *Messenger* (July 1918): 18.

Grimké, Charlotte Forten. *The Journals of Charlotte Forten Grimké*. Ed. Brenda Stevenson. New York: Oxford University Press, 1988.

Grosz, Elizabeth. *Sexual Subversions: Three French Feminists*. Sydney, Australia: Allen and Unwin, 1989.

Guthrie, Russell Dale. *Body Hot Spots: The Anatomy of Human Social Organs and Behavior.* New York: Van Nostrand Reinhold, 1976.

Guy-Sheftall, Beverly. *Daughters of Sorrow: Attitudes toward Black Women, 1880–1920.* New York: Carlson Publishing, 1990.

Hall, Stuart. "Cultural Identity and Cinematic Representation." *Framework 36* (Winter 1986): 68–82.

———. "Cultural Studies: Two Paradigms." *Media, Culture and Society 2* (1980): 57–72.

———. "Culture, the Media and the 'Ideological' Effect." In *Mass Communications and Society,* ed. James Curran, Michael Gurevitch, and Janet Woolacott, 315–348. London: Edward Arnold, 1977.

———. "Notes on Deconstructing 'the Popular.'" In *People's History and Socialist Theory,* ed. Ralph Samuel, 227–240. History Workshop Series. London: Routledge and Kegan Paul, 1981.

———. "The Rediscovery of 'Ideology': Return of the Repressed in Media Studies." In *Culture, Society and the Media,* ed. Michael Gurevitch, Tony Bennett, James Curran, and Janet Woolacott, 56–90. New York: Methuen, 1982.

Harlan, Louis R., and Raymond Smock, eds. *The Booker T. Washington Papers,* Vol. 11, *1911–1912.* Urbana: University of Illinois Press, 1981.

Harris, David. "The Mass Media: Politics and Popularity." In *From Class Struggle to the Politics of Pleasure: The Effects of Gramscianism on Cultural Studies,* 112–128. New York: Routledge, 1992.

hooks, bell. *Black Looks: Race and Representation.* Boston: South End Press, 1992.

———. "Straightening Our Hair." *Z Magazine* (Summer 1988): 14–18.

———. *Yearning: Race, Gender, and Cultural Politics.* Boston: South End Press, 1990.

Horton, James Oliver. "Freedom's Yoke: Gender Conventions Among Antebellum Free Blacks." *Feminist Studies 12* (Spring 1986): 8–20.

Hull, Gloria T., Patricia Bell Scott, and Barbara Smith, eds. *All The Women Are White, All The Blacks Are Men, But Some of Us Are Brave.* Old Westbury, N.Y.: Feminist Press, 1982.

Huyssen, Andreas. "Mass Culture as Woman: Modernism's Other." In *Studies in Entertainment: Critical Approaches to Mass Culture,* ed. Tania Modleski, 188–207. Bloomington and Indianapolis: Indiana University Press, 1986.

Jewell, K. Sue. *From Mammy to Miss America and Beyond: Cultural Imagery and the Shaping of U.S. Social Policy.* New York: Routledge, 1992.

Jhally, Sut. *The Codes of Advertising: Fetishism and the Political Economy of Meaning in the Consumer Society.* New York: Routledge, 1990.

Johnson, Abby, and Ronald Johnson. *Propoganda and Aesthetics: The Literary Politics of Afro-American Magazines in the Twentieth Century.* Boston: University of Massachusetts Press, 1979.

Jones, Jacqueline. *Labor of Love, Labor of Sorrow: Black Women, Work, and the Family from Slavery to the Present.* New York: Basic Books, 1985.

Jordan, Winthrop. *White over Black: American Attitudes toward the Negro, 1550–1812.* New York: Norton, 1968.

Joseph, Gloria, and Jill Lewis. *Common Differences: Conflicts in Black and White Feminist Perspectives.* Boston: South End Press, 1981.

Laclau, Ernesto, and Chantal Mouffe. *Hegemony and Socialist Strategy: Towards a Radical Democratic Politics.* London: Thetford Press, 1985.

Lears, T. J. Jackson. "The Rise of American Advertising." *Wilson Quarterly* 7 (Winter 1983): 156–167.

Lerner, Gerda. *Black Women in White America.* New York: Random House, 1973.

Levine, Lawrence W. *Black Culture and Black Consciousness: Afro-American Folk Thought from Slavery to Freedom.* New York: Oxford University Press, 1977.

Lipsitz, George. "Listening to Learn and Learning to Listen: Popular Culture, Cultural Theory, and American Studies." *American Quraterly* 42 (December 1990): 615–637.

Locke, Alain, ed. *The New Negro.* New York: Albert and Charles Boni, 1925.

McCracken, Ellen. *Decoding Women's Magazines: From Mademoiselle to Ms.* New York: St. Martin's Press, 1993.

Mcdowell, Deborah. "New Directions for Black Feminist Criticism." *Black American Literature Forum* 14 (Fall 1985): 153–162.

Marable, Manning. *How Capitalism Underdeveloped Black America.* Boston: South End Press, 1983.

Marchand, Roland. *Advertising the American Dream: Making Way For Modernity, 1920–1940.* Berkeley: University of California Press, 1985.

Martin, Waldo E., Jr. *The Mind of Frederick Douglass.* Chapel Hill: University of North Carolina Press, 1984.

Marwick, Arthur. *Beauty in History: Society, Politics, and Personal Appearance c. 1500 to the Present.* London: Thames and Hudson, 1988.

Mason, Eleanor, "Hot Irons and Black Nationalism." *Liberator* (May 1963): 12–15.

Massa, Ann. "Black Women in the 'White City.'" *Journal of American Studies* 8 (December 1974): 319–337.

Meier, August. *Negro Thought in America, 1880–1915: Racial Ideologies in the Age of Booker T. Washington.* Ann Arbor: University of Michigan Press, 1966.

Mitchell, Sally. *The Fallen Angel: Chasity, Class, and Women's Reading, 1835–1880.* Bowling Green, Ohio: Bowling Green University Popular Press, 1981.

Modleski, Tania. "Feminism and the Power of Intreptation: Some Critical Readings." In *Feminist Studies/Critical Studies,* ed. Teresa de Lauretis, 121–138. Bloomington: Indiana University Press, 1986.

Moore, Fred. "How to Keep Women at Home." *Colored American Magazine* 14 (January 1908): 7–8.

Moses, Jeremiah Wilson. "Domestic Feminism, Conservatism, Sex Roles, and Black Women's Clubs, 1863–1896." *Journal of Social and Behavioral Sciences* 24 (Fall 1978): 166–177.

Nicholson, Linda, ed. *Feminism and Postmodernism.* New York: Routledge, 1990.

Ohmann, Richard. "Where Did Mass Culture Come From? The Case of Magazines." *Berkshire Review* 16 (1981): 85–101.

Peiss, Kathy. *Cheap Amusements: Working Women and Leisure in Turn-of-the-Century New York.* Philadelphia: Temple University Press, 1986.

Penn, Irvine Garland. *The Afro-American Press and Its Editors.* Springfield, Mass.: Willey and Co., 1891.

Radway, Janice A. *Reading the Romance: Women, Patriarchy, and Popular Literature.* Chapel Hill: University of North Carolina Press, 1984.

Robinson, Cedric J. *Black Marxism: The Making of the Black Radical Tradition.* London: Zed Press, 1983.

Rudwick, Elliot M., and August Meier. "Black Man in the 'White City': Negroes and the Columbian Exposition, 1893." *Phylon* 26 (Winter 1965): 354–361.

Rushing, Andrea Benton. "Hair-Raising." *Feminist Studies* 14 (Summer 1988): 325–335.

Rydell, Robert W. "The World's Columbian Exposition, 1893: Racist Underpinnings of a Utopian Artifact." *Journal of American Culture* 1 (Summer 1978): 253–275.

Scott, Ann Firor. "Most Invisible of All: Black Women's Voluntary Associations." *Journal of Southern History* 1 (February 1990): 3–22.

Scruggs, Lawson. *Women of Distiction.* Raleigh: L. A. Scruggs, 1893.

Shevelow, Kathryn. "Fathers and Daughters: Women as Readers of the *Tattler.*" In *Gender and Reading: Essays on Readers, Texts, and Contexts,* ed. Elizabeth A. Flynn and Patrocinio P. Schweickart, 107–123. Baltimore: Johns Hopkins University Press, 1986.

———. *Women and Print Culture: The Construction of Femininity in the Early Periodical.* London: Routledge, 1989.

Spillers, Hortense. "Black/Female/Critic." *Women's Review of Books* 2 (September 1985): 9–10.

Sterling, Dorothy. *We Are Your Sisters: Black Women in the Nineteenth Centruy,* New York: Norton, 1984.

Stocking, George, Jr. *Race, Culture and Evolution.* New York: Free Press, 1968.

Tate, Greg. "Of Homegirl Goddesses and Geechee Women: The Africentric Cinema of Julie Dash." *Village Voice* (June 4, 1991): 72, 78.

Trachtenberg, Alan. *The Incorporation of America: Culture and Society in the Gilded Age.* New York: Hill and Wang, 1982.

Ussher, Jane M. *The Psychology of the Female Body.* New York: Routledge, 1989.

Wade-Gayles, Gloria. "The Making of a Permanent Afro." *Catalyst: A Magazine of Heart and Mind* (Summer 1988): 20–26.

———. *No Crystal Stair: Visions of Race and Sex in Black Women's Fiction.* New York: Pilgrim Press, 1984.

Walker, Alice, "Oppressed Hair Puts a Ceiling on the Brain." In Alice Walker, *Living By the Word,* 60–74. New York: Harcourt Brace Jovanovich, 1988.

Wallace, Michelle. *Invisibility Blues: From Pop to Theory.* New York: Verso, 1990.

Washington, Booker T., N. B. Wood, and Fannie Barrier Williams, eds. *A New Negro for a New Century.* Chicago, 1900.

Welch, Barbara. "Being-in-the-Body: A Reflection Upon American Self-Medication in Drug Advertising." Ph.D. dissertation, Univeristy of Iowa, 1984.

West, Cornel. "Marxist Theory and the Specificity of Afro-American Oppression." In *Marxism and the Interpretation of Culture,* ed. Cary Nelson and Lawrence Grossbert. Urbana: University of Illinois Press, 1988.

———. "The New Cultural Politics of Difference." In *Out There: Marginalization and Contemporary Cultures,* ed. Russell Ferguson et al., 19–39. New York: The New Museum of Contemporary Art, 1990.

White, Cynthia L. *Women's Magazines, 1693–1968.* London: Michael Joseph, 1970.

White, Deborah Gray. *Aren't I a Woman? Female Slaves in the Plantation South.* New York: Norton, 1985.

Williamson, Judith. *Decoding Advertisements: Ideology and Meaning in Advertising.* London and New York: Marion Boyars, 1978.

———. "Woman Is an Island: Femininity and Colonization." In *Studies in Entertainment: Critical Approaches to Mass Culture,* ed. Tania Modleski, 99–118. Bloomington and Indianapolis: Indiana University Press, 1986.

Willis, Susan. "I Shop Therefore I Am: Is There a Place for Afro-American Culture in Commodity Culture?" In *Changing Our*

Own Words: Essays on Criticsm, Theory, and Writing by Black Women, ed. Cheryl A. Wall, 173–195. New Brunswick, N.J.: Rutgers University Press, 1989.

Wilson, Elizabeth. *Adorned in Dreams: Fashion and Modernity.* Berkeley: University of California Press, 1985.

Wilson, William J. "White Is Beautiful." *Frederick Douglass' Paper* (March 11, 1853): 12–13.

Woodford, John. *The Strange Story of False Hair.* London: Routledge and Kegan Paul, 1971.

NEWSPAPERS

Chicago Defender (September, 18, 1915): 12.
Chicago Defender (May 1, 1915): 18.
Indianapolis Ledger (May 2, 1906): 10.
The New York Age (August 2, 1919): 5.
New York Age (August 2, 1910): 5.
New York Age (November 12, 1914): 15.
St. Louis Palladium (March 22, 1901): 6.
St. Louis Palladium (January 10, 1903): 8.
St. Louis Palladium (September 23, 1905): 8.
St. Louis Palladium (May 18, 1907): 22.

Index

About the Author

Noliwe M. Rooks is an assistant professor of English and the coordinator of African American Studies at the University of Missouri, Kansas City. She was the associate editor of *Paris Connections: African American Artists in Paris* and winner of a 1993 American Book Award.